A BEGINNER'S GUIDE TO THE

FOUR PSYCHIC CLAIR SENSES

*Clairvoyance, Clairaudience,
Claircognizance, Clairsentience*

KEVIN HUNTER

WARRIOR OF LIGHT PRESS
Los Angeles, California

Warrior of Light Press
www.kevin-hunter.com

Body, Mind & Spirit/Angels & Guides
Inspiration & Personal Growth

Some content in the *Four Psychic Clair Senses* book is featured in *Spirit Guides and Angels*, *Ignite Your Inner Life Force*, *Awaken Your Creative Spirit*, and *Warrior of Light* with a great deal of added new material threaded throughout that is not featured anywhere else.

Acknowledgements

Thank you to my Spirit team council of Guides, Angels, Archangels, and Saints. Thank you also to Archangels Michael, Gabriel, Uriel, and Zadkiel for your endless reservoir of support, guidance, and messages.

Chapters

Warrior of Light
pocket book series

Spirit Guides and Angels
How I Communicate with Heaven

Soul Mates and Twin Flames
Attracting in Love, Friendships and the Human Heart

Divine Messages for Humanity
Channeled Communication from the Other Side on Death, the Afterlife, the Ego, Prejudices, Prayer and the Power of Love

Raising Your Vibration
Fine Tune Your Body & Soul to Receive Messages from Heaven

Connecting with the Archangels

The Seven Deadly Sins
A Modern Day Interpretation of Humanity's Toxic Challenges with a Practical Spiritual Twist

Love Party of One
Surviving the Pitfalls of Dating and Relationships in a Loveless World

A Beginner's Guide to the
Four Psychic Clair Senses
Clairvoyance, Clairaudience, Claircognizance, Clairsentience

Introduction

Over the years, I would bring up the topic of clair channels with people new to spiritual concepts. The responses were the same, "What is that?" After explaining it to them, they would then profess to having heard of and knowing about Clairvoyance, but had not heard of the others. As I discussed the various clair channels with them, they would grow excited to hear about the other clairs that exist and realize they too have received unexplained psychic hits. They would become ecstatic in learning that they have psychic capabilities just as anyone else does on the planet, but hadn't paid much attention to it before. They were under the impression that only a special group of chosen people are granted psychic capabilities. As they looked back to notice the synchronicities in their life, they came to the realization that they are psychic too! This was the ultimate reasoning behind the gestation of this book. It was to offer a basic beginner's guide discussing the four core clair psychic channels that everyone has built into their soul. This is to help you pay more attention to it and how it can help you while moving along your Earthly journey. I am psychic, and so are you! Being in tune to the four psychic clair senses can help you navigate through your life much more efficiently. It makes up for a smoother ride when you are aware of what it means to have Clairvoyance, Clairaudience, Claircognizance, and Clairsentience. This book is for you at the start of your spiritual awareness journey.

Author's Note

All *Warrior of Light* books are infused with practical messages and guidance that my Spirit team has taught and shared with me revolving around many different topics. The main goal is to fine tune your body, mind, and soul. This improves humanity one person at a time. You are a Divine communicator and perfectly adjusted and capable of receiving messages from Heaven. This is for your benefit in order to live a happier, richer life. You may not be stress free, but it will help train you to glide through it more efficiently. It is your individual responsibility to respect yourself and this planet while on your journey here.

The messages and information enclosed in this and all of the *Warrior of Light* books may be in my own words, but they do not come from me. They come from God, the Holy Spirit, my Spirit team of guides, angels and sometimes certain Archangels and Saints. I am merely the liaison or messenger in delivering and interpreting the intentions of what they wish to communicate. They love that I talk about them and share this stuff as it gets other people to work with them too!

There is one main hierarchy Saint who works with me leading the pack. His name is Nathaniel. He is often brutally truthful and forceful, as he does not mince words. There may be topics in this and my other books that might bother you or make you uncomfortable. He asks that you examine the underlying cause of this discomfort and come to terms with the fear attached. He cuts right to the heart of humanity without apology. I have learned quite a bit from him while adopting his ideology, which is Heaven's philosophy as a whole.

I am one with the Holy Spirit and have many Spirit Guides and Angels around me. As my connections to the other side grew to be daily over the course of my life, more of them joined in behind the others. I have often seen, sensed, heard, and been privy to the dozens of magnificent lights that crowd around me on occasion.

If I use the word "He" when pertaining to God, this does not mean that I am advocating that He is a male. Simply replace the word, "He" with one you are comfortable using to identify God for you to be. This goes for any gender I use as examples. When I say, "spirit team", I am referring to a team of 'Guides and Angels'.

The purpose of the *Warrior of Light* books is to empower and help you improve yourself, your life, and humanity as a whole. It does not matter if you are a beginner or well versed in the subject matter. There may be something that reminds you of something you already know or something that you were unaware of. We all have much to share with one another, as we are all one in the end. This book and all of the *Warrior of Light* series of books contain information and directions on how to reach the place where you can be a fine tuned instrument to receive your own messages from your own Spirit team.

Some of my personal stories are infused and sprinkled throughout. This is in order for you to see how it works effectively for me. With some of my methods, you may gain additional insight, knowledge, or inspiration. It may prompt you to recall incidents where you were receiving heavenly messages in your own life. There are helpful ways that you can improve your existence and have a connection with Heaven throughout this book. Doing so will greatly transform yourself in all ways allowing you to attract wonderful circumstances at higher levels and live a happier more content life.

~ Kevin Hunter

A BEGINNER'S GUIDE TO THE
FOUR PSYCHIC
CLAIR SENSES

Chapter One

THE FOUR PSYCHIC CLAIR SENSES

My Spirit team council of Guides, Angels, Archangels, and Saints have been around me for as long as I can remember, talking as loud as a human being would if they were standing next to me. I never needed a brick wall to fall on me to be 100% aware of their presence. It's not like they suddenly showed up one day, because they have been indefinitely present since I was conscious.

From the perspective of a child, I knew then without questioning it that there were others around me that cannot be seen through one's physical eyes. These beings move about with me like a private entourage going wherever I go. I've forever been cognizant that they connect from another dimension guiding me, warning me, telling me things that were later coming true. They work with me as if they are a staff I personally hired for this gig. All of that confirmed to me from an early age that the Earth plane is just some bizarre alternate Universe structured in a way that is similar to a school that houses both students and teachers. It's why I've viewed world events differently than the masses do and instead through the lens of the "others".

Over the course of my life, whether in school or professional endeavors, instructors or superiors would say, "I'd like to hear what Kevin has to say. Not to put you on the spot, but your point of view tends to typically be different than everyone else's. It makes one consider the alternative and see things in another light."

There are more than one being that communicates with me. They all mostly stand to my left. Sometimes they communicate separately and other times in unison. They alternate or take turns if one of the others are temporarily busy or have stepped away. I knew from an early age they were present to assist me through the rapid turbulently abusive evolving process I endured for decades. They work with me as I move about on my Earthly path to ensure all of my needs are met. This is to guarantee that I'm in a space of serenity as much as possible in order to fulfill my purpose. They understand that when you are taken care of without worry, then you are able to focus on higher priorities.

I knew without questioning it that my Spirit team was on my side like an unconditional best friend. They are the closest thing to family and have never given the illusion of being against me. This is because they are highly trained wise enlightened ones who don't fall into the darkness of ego. They continuously have my highest self's purpose and interests at heart. Like all beings in the spirit world, they know my every thought and move before I've made it, as well as yours.

As a child, there was no name for them or a word to describe how I was hearing them. I also never questioned it, but I was consciously aware that they were in a different plane or dimension, but unable to break through that barrier to communicate with me at times. Labels never crossed my mind as to who they are or where they were communicating with me from. It did not occur to me that it was a place that some people on Earth refer to as Heaven, while others call it the spirit world, other side, or whatever. There were no labels or words for it growing up. It never crossed my mind and nor did I think twice about it. It just was and is understood without second guessing it. Now I use labels to describe it so that people know what I'm talking about, but in reality it was a telepathic knowing who they were without trying to find a word for it.

Growing up, I viewed them as being a highly advanced and intelligent council of wise ones that seemed centuries older than I from the point of view of a human eight year old boy. What I didn't realize until much later was that I was just as old as they were, and that I previously called on them to work with me before I entered another Earthly life to eventually assume the role of a teacher. This was one I was resistant on for a few decades until I finally snapped out of that and realized I was already a teacher whether I preferred to be or not. It is impossible to deny my Wise One heritage.

I assumed everyone had the same deal and that they were hearing voices that were not their ego too, but I later discovered that most were not aware of it at all on any level. It stunned me initially to know that a vast enormous amount of people on the planet were that disconnected from Spirit. This was unheard of to me and further isolated me even more from the general masses.

I don't know any other life and cannot imagine living life with that kind of a disconnect or a lack of awareness. If I didn't feel like I was different before that point, then I most definitely did after coming to the realization that there are quite a number of people on the planet who are indeed disconnected from spirit. This has been evident all throughout history, throughout all of the fighting, antagonism, complaining, wars, hatred, and so on. Those guilty of those traits are not connected to Spirit. Earth is a divided planet filled with disengaged souls as if God just dumped the scraps on it and gave them free reign to destroy it the way a child destroys their bedroom. Being misanthropic is a clear cut Wise One trait, because they know the greatness that a soul is capable of, but the soul just lost its way by falling into the ego's attraction to the gutter of superficiality.

No one who has been paying any attention can deny that Earth has been in a permanent state of disarray at the hands of corrupt human souls. The higher your psychic awareness is, then the more conscious you are of the disintegrating state of the planet. You cannot be in denial of this reality. You can be optimistic that there is serenity up ahead for life on Earth, which is why many sensitive strong loving souls incarnate into an Earthly life. It is in order to help move humanity along towards that goal. The struggle for them is that Earth is not an easy place for them to live on. They are aware of Earth's decay and have great distaste over the toxic behavior of humanity as a whole. When you are conscious of that feeling, then that is a sign that you are called on here to rise up and fight to bring love to Earth. You are an Earth Angel with the goal to help raise the consciousness of all souls back into its original state of being that is love.

I've had to find ways to explain throughout some of my books how all souls have the ability to connect with spirit, which is by incorporating healthy positive life changes. Many human beings have been recalling how they have been picking up on Heavenly communication as Earthly life progresses. In that respect, perception and awareness is gradually expanding, but just not fast enough. It would speed things along if metaphysical concepts were widely and Universally accepted and became a mandatory requirement in grade school. The masses are still stuck in the extremism of either taking the word of the Bible verbatim to the opposite extreme of having no belief system at all. It is challenging for them to move themselves into the middle of the road where balance is in order to test and assess the possibilities that exist within their soul.

There are a surplus of spirit beings in the numerous heavenly realms that exist beyond the Earthly physical plane. These spirits include angels, guides, archangels, spirit guides, guardian angels, realm spirits, saints, ascended masters, and deceased loved ones. The word *spirit* is used in order to assist human beings in deciphering the difference between a physical human being as opposed to someone who has crossed over and how that being appears to others. Those on the other side are not spirits in the sense that one believes them to be such as transparent and hollow the way the ghosts look in Disneyland's Haunted Mansion. Even through a clairvoyant's peripheral vision, the spirit may appear transparent due to the veil that separates the Earth and Spirit plane.

Spirits on the other side are a spirit in the same way that a human being is essentially a spirit, but living in a temporary physical body. The spirit on the other side can easily morph into how they choose to appear, whether that be physically whole, to a spirit translucent form, or to a light source, and so on.

There are no limitations beyond the physical world. The freedom to appear how one chooses back home on the other side is limitless. The only thing that doesn't change is the soul's consciousness. The soul's consciousness grows and evolves, but the essence of that soul remains relatively the same, which at its core is all love. If the soul's consciousness hasn't evolved, then it goes through specific training that includes incarnating into an Earthly life. Earthly life is made up of teachers and students in various levels of spirit evolvement.

There are a great many human souls living an Earthly life that do not change or evolve rapidly in one lifetime, so they re-incarnate for additional lifetimes in order to learn lessons and evolve their consciousness. There are also a great many souls who are evolving much more rapidly than others on Earth. They are the ones that are easy to detect. They might have started out in a childhood filled with dysfunction, abuse, or limitations, but by the time they reached adulthood they come off as a different person entirely having risen above it and contributed something positive towards assisting humanity in some way. This might be in the form of shining their ever loving bright light on those who need to be lifted up. The rough experiences they endured enabled them to evolve more rapidly than the average baby soul living an Earthly life. The resistance the evolved soul faced from others strengthened them into a fighter for the greater good.

Many evolved souls are ultra-sensitive to the point that they feel every nuance around them and therefore find it challenging to be around people except for a select chosen few, most of which make up their soul family. They avoid crowds when possible, and take on a neutral balanced view of human life. This means they don't get caught up in any form of gossip media or consistent complaining energy surrounding politics, both of which are the most dangerous toxic attractors to the human ego today. They know that by falling into fear, anger, and gossip is to not be operating from God, which sees all life from the perspective of an unconditional loving parent.

The exception to this is if the soul is working hard to get other souls to move away from negative energy and avoid falling into the epicenter of its toxicity. The other exception are those working within the human physical system in order to take positive action that provides optimistic change. There is nothing angelic or spiritual about constantly complaining and bickering negatively on social media about political laws enacted. This leaves the number of highly evolved souls to be in the lower ranges, since the majority of the masses fall easily into the deception of its physical surroundings.

Before I hit adulthood, I witnessed others who weren't the greatest compassionate people as children and teenagers. They might have been the abrasive bully who was rebellious, abusive, or causing trouble, but then I ran into them as adults and they were completely different people appearing as intelligent, compassionate, loving, upstanding souls with an enormous light around them that wasn't there before. This is an example of a rapid growing soul able to raise their consciousness quicker than the speed of light.

The brighter the light is around you, then the easier it is to communicate with those on the other side. This light acts as a portal to connect with your Spirit team made up of one Spirit Guide and one Guardian Angel. They are with you from your Earthly birth until your Earthly death. Upon your human death is when you pass on through the tunnel doorway back home to stand face to face with your Spirit team. Those who work with angels, guides, or any being in Heaven on a grander level tend to have more spirit beings around working with them. Those who have larger purposes to help move humanity forward towards the ultimate goal that is love, will also have more guides around helping them with this purpose.

Guides and angels also join you for specific purposes in your practical life and then they move on. A guide may be assigned to help someone on Earth cross paths with their various soul mates, including the love oriented mate. This particular guide will remain with that person until the two people are in a relationship. It doesn't matter if it takes the guide six months or six years. The guide will remain with that person until the connection has been made. There are also guides who will help a couple strengthen their connection if it is requested by one or both partners. There are also guides to help someone find a new place to live or find an Earthly job in order to survive physically on the planet and pay for human necessities such as food, housing, clothing, etc. The guide that offers that extra assistance will stay with the person until the quest is fulfilled, then the guide moves onto other activities of its choice.

It doesn't matter if the human being is an atheist, non-believer, or not very spiritual. They are not discriminated against by Heaven due to their inability to sense, hear, know, or see any soul or spirit presence of life beyond Earth.

There are numerous enlightened beings residing in a variety of spirit realms to assist human souls that request their help. All in Heaven cannot email you or pick up the phone and call you, therefore they use other varying means and methods to communicate with you called *clair channels* (clear communication). These clairs are your crystal clear etheric senses used to communicate with any being in the spirit realms. The clairs enable you to receive heavenly messages, guidance, and information to positively assist you or another along your Earthly journey. The clair channels are much like the channels one would use to switch on a television or a radio to a channel that you feel most comfortable with. You are a walking divination tool that allows you to communicate with Spirit.

The clair channels are not visible to the physical eyes. They are located within every soul that exists whether human, animal, or any species. They are the core channels that all souls have, which also means that every human soul that exists on Earth is immensely psychic regardless if they believe in psychic phenomena or not. Every soul is picking up on psychic input information, even if they are completely unaware that they are. That is until someone points it out causing a big reaction. "Oh, I didn't realize that's what I was doing!"

The clair channels are connected to your etheric senses, which are also connected to your energy Chakras. Your senses are Divine communication tools with Heaven, the Other Side, or the Spirit World. It doesn't matter what you call the other world as it is all the same place regardless. This is the same as all paths leading to God.

Your senses, chakras, and over all well-being needs to be kept clean of debris and trash that blocks the communication line with God. The more negative you are, then the more clogged your *clairs* become. This is why spiritual practitioners insist on living as joyful and toxic free of a life as you can manage.

You are born with natural heightened crystal clear channels of communication with the other side built into your soul. When you absorb any form of negativity, then this creates a block preventing you from picking up on psychic input. The negativity you absorb includes words, thoughts, and feelings. This also includes negative words you hear from others around you. You may be in a perfect state of reception, but if you're around toxic people or even reading toxic posts on social media or on gossip news sites, then this can and will dim the light around you causing lower psychic input.

What you consume into your body also plays a part in how loud or quiet your psychic *clair* channels are. This includes the kind of food or drinks you ingest. There is that true saying that states, "You are what you eat." If you eat a heavy meal, you may have a difficult time picking up on the Divine messages from the other side for hours afterwards. If you get wasted drunk on a bottle of wine, then this will also dim the communication line. If you're so drunk or high that you don't remember what you're doing or saying, or what someone else did or said, then that also means you won't pick up on the messages coming in from your Spirit team too.

There have been terrorist attacks that have taken place at bars and clubs such as the historical ones in Paris, France or Orlando, Florida. If many of the patrons were consuming tons of alcohol, then it is unlikely they were picking up on the warnings from their guides beforehand that they should get out of there. Their senses were blocked preventing the input of psychic guidance. This isn't said as a form of judgment, or that anyone asked for it, and nor is it suggesting that you're not allowed to have an alcoholic drink. On the contrary, it is pointing out what can or will dim the psychic communication line with the other side. This same communication line is what can warn you of danger or to pay attention to something.

Trust me on occasion I have enjoyed my cold beer at a beach BBQ with close friends on a hot summer day and classic rock music blasting, or a glass of red wine with a lover overlooking a serene vineyard, but I'm also aware that it is dimming the spirit communication line in that instant. I'll need to follow up my toxic fun with re-centering my state of being in order to be a fine tuned divination tool again. No one is trying to spoil your fun as the angels are huge advocates for letting loose and relaxing, but they also know what can happen when something is overdone for long periods of time.

I'm fully aware of when I'm dimming the communication line and when I'm in a full state of psychic reception. I learned this the hard way as I moved into my early 20's when I was already a full blown partying drinker, drug user, and cigarette smoker. You name it and I probably did it or tried it. I realized that I was straining to hear the voices of my Spirit team through the thud haze of toxins in those days. Through my lifetime of personal experiences, I became exceptionally adept at detecting what was lowering the Divine communication and what was raising it. I worked hard to eliminate or dissolve what was not only destroying my well-being, but also turning the volume down in my psychic channels. The same can be said about anyone who is experiencing a block created at their own hands by diving into anything negative or toxic in any form. When you're distracted by the happenings in practical life, then you're distracted from receiving heavenly messages.

You've likely heard about children talking to angels or what some perceive to be imaginary friends that no one else can see. Unfortunately, some adults thrash and shatter that belief in those children by saying, "That's just your imaginary friend."

These invented friends are not always as imaginary as a jaded adult might believe. We've seen this in Hollywood films surrounding psychic phenomena. Usually it's a horror or thriller film where the spirit has infiltrated itself around the child. The parent of the child tends to catch the child talking to him/herself.

"Who were you talking to honey?"

The child says, "That's my friend, Bob."

The jaded disconnected parent has a perplexed confused look not knowing what to make of it. A spiritually based parent would have picked up on it right away and talked with the child immediately about this gift they have. Whereas the cynical parent would have shattered this idea causing a block for the child who later grows up not having any connection at all. Naturally, in these movies it turns out to be a much bigger sinister spirit that causes all sorts of issues in that home. This is where Hollywood is moving more into fantasy entertainment, since that is not likely to happen in reality. One is more likely to attract in negative energy from another human being, before it attracts in a negative spirit into its vicinity. Although it is true that some negative entities who have not crossed over into the Light for various reasons can attach itself onto a living being. You would know this were the case if you were constantly miserable or falling into toxic addictions unable to come out of it. What would make this unusual is if this behavior is unusual to your everyday life and no other sources triggered the addiction.

You can call upon your Spirit team as well as the Archangel Michael to clear you of any toxins that have latched itself onto your aura. All Archangels are unlimited and can be with anyone who calls on them.

You are born with heightened functioning clair senses within your soul, but there are typically one or two clairs that are more dominant in you than others. These clair senses are your psychic senses.

Over time your clair channels dim and darken due to things such as: Blocks created by society, a heavy interest in the material world, domination of your ego, consumption of negative substances, and poor lifestyle choices. These are some of the predominant situations that clog your clair channels. When your clair channels are clogged, then this prevents you from communicating or even knowing that you are receiving messages and guidance from Heaven.

When any spirit being in Heaven communicates with you, the tone is direct, full of love, and uplifting, even if they are warning you of danger. They communicate firmly, while your ego communicates with uncertainty, anger, or any other disapproving emotion. Your Spirit team will never advise you to do something that ends up hurting you or someone else. This can be something such as developing a sudden urge to recklessly pack up and move away to another city all of a sudden. It can be leaving a soul mate connection that was intended for you in order to go after someone else. Notice around you whom it might hurt including yourself. Rash decisions typically tend to come from the ego since the ego is impatient. It believes the grass is greener elsewhere, but where it currently is. It later discovers it acted impulsively only to find that they are still unhappy or life has fallen into an endless downward spiral.

I've witnessed countless incidents where others have continuously made impulsive decisions that end up being regrettable to the person in the end. It takes them downward, rather than upward.

Before they know it, years have passed and they're no closer to what they want than where they started. The more you work with your Spirit team, then the better you get at deciphering what is your Spirit team and your higher self, and what is your ego or lower self.

Your Spirit Guide, Guardian Angel, God, or any entity or spirit communicates with you through your senses. Your senses are not to be confused with your physical senses, but these senses are interwoven between your physical body and your soul. These senses are your clairs. It is being a clear channel with the other side. I am hugely in touch with my Spirit team and have been for as long as I can remember. I am in constant communication from morning until night, on and off throughout each day. There is rarely a moment when I'm not in connection with them. They sift in and out randomly every hour through my day and night while in dream state. It's kind of like traveling around with my own spirit entourage. I appear distracted at times for that reason too. There are over a dozen clair points in your soul, but there are four primary clairs.

The four basic Clair channels are:

Clairvoyance (clear seeing)
Clairaudience (clear hearing)
Clairsentience (clear feeling)
Claircognizance (clear knowing)

It takes work and a lifestyle change to keep the clairs open since the clear senses can dim or close.

Your clairs are also considered to be extra sensory perception, because the clair senses reach places beyond what your physical senses are able to do. You hear the voices of spirit, but your physical ears are not hearing them. It is your spirit/soul senses that hear them. The *extra sensory* part of the equation is the *extra sense* that is beyond the physical.

It is assumed that someone with psychic abilities is gifted, but these gifts have been given to every living soul. No one is more special than anyone else where psychic abilities are concerned. Everyone is psychic and has the ability to connect with the other side. Some connect easier than others or in different ways than someone else does. That person might have done the work to re-open their clair senses, or they live a life that has minimal blocks in their environment. While the other case is they are naturally sensitive and in tune to the vibrations coming in from beyond.

All souls have psychic gifts, but you're not paying attention to this input of information if you are buried deep into the physical world. Consumed by the materially based physical world comes with an array of blocks that reduces your psychic gifts. The good news is that one's psychic gifts never go away. They might dim or darken, but they're accessible to anyone who chooses to re-awaken that part of their soul. Receiving Divine guidance can help your life in immense ways. It can assist you in all aspects of your life from finding a love partner, to the right job, moving through your life purpose, locating a new home dwelling, or through a warning that prevents you from danger or making a wrong move. Having a Spirit team may not remove some of the stresses that pop up in daily life, but it can certainly help you to move past it more efficiently than not having that connection.

Your Spirit team will not give you every single answer you require, since they will not live your life for you. There is some information that is not given until the right time, or there are certain things you need to be enlightened about on your own. This also goes for the incredibly gifted or the spiritual heavenly teachers of the world who are also not exempt from challenges placed on their path. They are in a human body and living a physical life after all, and with that challenges will arise.

The upcoming chapters focus on each of the four basic clairs that all souls have. It gives examples and scenarios of what they are, how I've picked up on messages, and much more. Read the basic descriptions of the four core clairs coming up in order to pinpoint what best describes you and to have a better understanding of what they are and how they work.

You might find that a description explains a clair that you have, but then you may protest, "I don't have that clair." You may find that you have all four clairs, which would not be unusual because you, like everyone else, all have these clair points within your soul.

The descriptions discussed include what each

clair is as well as some personal examples of how I receive messages. This is in order to help you detect any similarities that remind you of when you were or are actually picking up on psychic input, but didn't realize it at the time.

If you feel you do not have any of the clairs, then that just means that you're experiencing a block because you have all clair points within you. Consider studying more up on a particular clair and how to develop and open it up. It's already there as it's a part of you, but it just needs to be worked out. It's the same way someone who goes to the gym regularly to build muscle. If they suddenly stopped going, then the muscle would lessen over time. Clairs work in that same respect. You treat it like a muscle that needs to be built, strengthened, and taken care of. Your physical body can build muscle or tone when you exercise. Your clair channels work in the same way. When you exercise a clair, then you build its muscle over time. From that point, you do the work out maintenance as you would if you were exercising regularly to strengthen and maintain your physical body and overall health.

Many resort to meditation or sitting in silence to awaken their psychic connection. The reason this is effective is it helps in relaxing you. It's the relaxing technique that helps awaken and open up your clair channels. When you're under stress or buried in any kind of negative emotion, then this creates a block preventing any psychic input.

Chapter Two

CLAIRVOYANCE

*C*lairvoyance means *clear seeing* or *clear viewing*. It is one of the most well-known clair channels even by those who do not protest to be a believer of anything beyond the Earthly physical plane. There are still some myths and false assumptions that many have about clairvoyance. One of them being that only a select number of special people have the gift of clairvoyance. Every soul has all of the clair senses within them regardless if they are aware of it or not.

One of the many ways that your Spirit team communicates with you is by transmitting visual moving pictures through your mind's eye, which is sometimes called the Third Eye. The Third Eye is invisible to the naked eye, which are your two physical eyes. The Third Eye is located between your physical eyes, but turned on its side.

The visual images or moving pictures are

played through your clairvoyant channel, which acts as a projector. This projector is your Third Eye projecting images back to you. These visuals might contain a premonition of what's to come, what's already happened, or what is currently taking place. Sometimes the visuals might have no rhyme or reason at first, but they are important to remember as it could later be the answer to a prayer or question for yourself or another on a matter. I hesitate to say 'important matter', because I receive various clairvoyant cues throughout each day, some of which are trivial, insignificant, and not major life altering messages. They are at times random images that sift in front of me as if I'm watching a film, then that image later shows up in real time.

Those that have strong Clairvoyance can see spirits as if they are standing in front of them. Those spirits are not necessarily whole and three dimensional like other human beings, but instead appear opaque or translucent. Spirits are in whole form back home on the other side. The reason they appear translucent to a clairvoyant on the Earth plane is due to the etheric barrier located between the Earth dimension and the next spirit dimension. The spirit dimension runs parallel along the Earth dimension three feet above it. There is a barrier in between which causes the image of a spirit coming through to appear hazy, distorted, or hollow. This is due to the heavy dense atmosphere that creates a thicker barrier between both planes.

Some people expect to see a spirit standing in front of them whole and in the flesh the way it's depicted in movies or as if it's a human person

21

standing directly in front of them, but this is usually not the case. You can see the spirit when you close your physical eyes in order to open up and peer out of your Third Eye. As you gradually excel with seeing things beyond the physical life through your Third Eye, then you may find you no longer have to close your physical eyes in order to peer through your Third Eye. There are a great deal of practicing Mediums that will choose to close their physical eyes when they are conducting a reading. This is so that they're not distracted by what's in front of them in the physical world. They can focus primarily through their Third Eye.

The Third Eye is an incredible device within your soul that enables you to see a deceased loved one, a spirit on the other side, an angel, a guide, or any being at all. Seeing a spirit clairvoyantly does not necessarily mean seeing them directly in front of you with your physical eyes open. It is closing your physical eyes with the intention that you will open up your Third Eye in order to see an angel, guide, or any other Divine Heavenly being.

The Third Eye is a part of every soul enabling you to effortlessly communicate beyond the physical means of communicating. It assists in giving you a stronger connection with your true home in Heaven. It is to help connect you with God, a higher vibrational being, your soul family, spirit guides, angels, or a loved one who has passed on. It is to help you positively move along comfortably throughout your Earthly life. It doesn't mean you will be problem or stress free, but it does strengthen you to be able to glide over those circumstances easier than if you did not have that connection. I've found over the decades that those who have the lowest spiritual connection tend to be more negative or absorbed in drama on a higher scale than those with a spiritual connection.

When you have a stronger connection with Heaven, then your perception of human life is altered for the better. You realize that the drama that the ego in human kind conjures up has no truth in long term reality. It only serves as a distraction to prevent you from moving forward on your path. It is safe to say that when you have a strong connection with the other side, then your soul naturally shuns all forms of negativity or drama around you in the physical world.

One of the reasons that people have a tough time becoming more psychic is due to wanting it so badly. When you try too hard at anything, then this blocks the results. All of this is connected to fear. Fear that you won't pick up on anything, so you strain and push to get something. When you get frustrated and annoyed that you're picking up on nothing, then that dims and blocks the psychic capabilities even more. Let go of the strong desire to be psychic and allow it to flow naturally.

The other reason some have a tough time with making a psychic connection is they don't have faith or believe in anything spiritual or metaphysical. Having some measure of skepticism is understandable and harmless, but when that skepticism moves to the rigid unbending belief system of atheism, then there isn't enough of an open mind within that soul to allow even the tiniest light to flow and break through the clairs that would crack it wide open with psychic hits.

It is not necessary to close your physical eyes in order to clairvoyantly see a spirit being, but if you're new to clairvoyance you may find it to be less challenging to start off that way. Eventually it grows easier where you can see what is intended to be seen while your physical eyes are open. Not everyone sees spirits in the same way. Some may see them in physical form, others may see them as lights and sparkles, while the rest may see them in the shape of angels, or however the spirit chooses to appear for that person. When I say spirit, this means any and all in Heaven, whether it is an angel, guide, archangel, saint, departed loved one, realm soul, or heavenly being.

If you are someone who has vivid dreams, which you recall long after you've woken up from sleep, then this is a sign that you have clairvoyant abilities. Clairvoyance includes having prophetic dreams where the images revealed in the dream can point to messages, guidance, or information pertaining to what you need to know about something or someone. It can offer a warning to avoid someone who is not of high integrity, or it can be telling you of something good coming into your life such as a romantic partner or a great job. Those who tend to recall their dreams or who have super vivid dreams may have a higher degree of Clairvoyance.

When I was five year old, I was Clairvoyantly seeing images of people that sometimes appeared scary through the eyes of a child. I noticed spirits walking out of the physical plane and into a doorway leading into the spirit plane. In the middle of the night at that same age, I awoke to see a strange man walking out of my bedroom. My heart beat fast not knowing who or what that was. The next minute I was standing at the foot of my mother's bed in the dark.

Dead tired she asked, "What is it?"

I looked down and noticed another visual of someone under her bed smiling at me. Trying to find the right words as a child to communicate that I was pretty sure I was seeing dead people was difficult because I didn't know what or who I was seeing.

I said, "There's someone in the house."

She'd say, "There's no one here. It's just your imagination."

As a Claircognizant, I did not buy this response. I chose to keep it to myself knowing I would not get anywhere trying to convince an adult of something that is real and not imaginary.

Clairvoyant messages delivered can come to you in many ways including in your dreams. In a vivid dream, I was wandering through what appeared to be an upper scale mall that one might find in a fancy Las Vegas Hotel. There was a spirit in a long black robe floating high in the air in the distance. The robe it was wearing also had a hoodie pulled over its skeleton head to reveal hollow eyes. It looked like the "Day of the Dead" artwork that one would find depicted in certain Mexican art. Spotting it knowing this was no friend I mumbled, "Uh-oh".

The Spirit was alerted to my words and turned its head and looked right through me. He accelerated his speed and quickly flew in the air around the gorgeous gold fountain in the center of the mall and headed directly towards me. I turned to run, but in dreams you do not always run, move, or get far when being chased. Unable to move I was paralyzed with a heaviness brought on out of fear. The spirit landed in front of me pulling out a long spear. He held it up and stabbed me in the stomach with it. The pain was sharp causing me to sense every bit of it as I jolted awake in the Earth plane. The pain continued long after I awoke and then evaporated to a good degree until I felt nothing. It reminded me of the horror movie, *The Nightmare on Elm Street*, where something bad happens to you in the dream and you take it out feeling it with you as you wake up.

Afterwards, I lit some Sage incense leaves to clear my space. The Sage smoke latches onto the negative energies and carries it away outside. Connecting with my guides afterwards I discovered that the spirit was not a demon spirit that I invited in. It was me! It was my fear that manifested this false entity. The spirit stabbed me in the stomach. Your stomach area is the spot where your inner power resides. My Spirit team explained that I was giving my power away to others and needed to take it back. I was also urged to stop with the ego infested fears and worries going on at that time in my life as they were unfounded. I closed my eyes invoking a blast of bright white light from the other side that took over that area in my body and the pain soon evaporated.

This clairvoyant example was not showing me a crystal clear visual of what was to come or a vision of the past. Sometimes the messages you receive through your clair channels need some deciphering or decoding. You might have to do a little detective work to discover what your Spirit team is relaying to you. This is specifically with clairvoyance, since the clairvoyant images may come through for you as symbols, signs, numbers, or visuals that might seem as if they have nothing to do with anything.

Clairvoyance is receiving visual images, cues, or impressions through your mind's eye. Spirit communication is being brought to you through a moving visual picture played through your Third Eye. The significance of the illustration does not always mean what is being shown to you. It is up to you to decipher what the message is supposed to be about. For example, you are asleep having a dream where you are walking the streets at night. There are hundreds of snakes and cobras moving about around you attacking everyone except you. As a clairvoyant, it's your goal to translate what this moving image is supposed to mean, because it's highly unlikely that this is an image showing you of what's to come. It can mean that you're a rising successful star in your profession who is untouchable, but this is not met without enemies. There is someone or a group of people who are or will be jealous of you. This could be one way to interpret the dream of the snakes attacking everyone around except you. Typically, when one reaches a certain level of success, then there will be naysayers around attempting to pull that person down. This resistance should make you stronger.

The darkness of ego falls effortlessly into one of the deadly sins of envy by despising confidence and success achieved in others. A high vibrational spirit being in Heaven would never be jealous or envious of someone's achievements, since positively triumphing is applauded on the other side. This is the case even if a member of the public doesn't care for that person. Any personal anger or distaste towards that artist comes from the darkness of ego, since high vibrational beings only exude love. Many witness this envy some have with popular artists, actors, singers, political candidates, authors, and all those who are propelled into public domain in some form. There is also the saying that you know you've made it when people are attacking you.

You have clairvoyance if you also see spirits from the other side. It looks as if they're in front of you or to the side of you. They don't look like actual physical people, which is the way they're portrayed in some Hollywood films. They look more opaque or translucent. You may see them as lights or sparkling lights in your peripheral vision. The sparkles of lights one sees through clairvoyance in their peripheral vision can be any spirit being on the other side, including angels or departed loved ones. Angels have a higher vibration over flowing love presence. Their lights are stronger and brighter than a departed loved one.

For some, your consciousness will block your

abilities to see spirits for fear of seeing a deceased spirit looking the way they had when they passed away. They might have died a violent death such as a murder or car accident. The spirit is fine and doesn't look like that on the other side, but they can appear how they choose to a human soul. This sometimes includes how they looked when they died or the age they passed away. If they died a violent death, then they might appear that way to be recognizable to you.

Someone's grandfather passed away at 92 years old, but when he crossed over he appears in top form looking like a young 25-34 year old human being. He might appear 92 years old in human years to a psychic Medium in order for that Medium to relay what is coming through in a reading for someone. You might not know who the Medium was talking about if your grandfather appeared the way he did at 25 years old. He would look significantly different if he appears as he is on the other side.

Clairvoyant messages can come in the disguise of symbols, numbers, colors, letters, words, and pictures that may have a meaning to you or someone else. It can be something from the past, the present, or future. Those who have clairvoyance have a tendency to daydream. These daydreams may be random or they may be images of what's happened, what's happening, or what's to come. They see their own future as if it's a vision board of what is to take place at some point. When someone tells a clairvoyant friend a story, the clairvoyant is living the story as if it's happening to them personally. They see the story as if they are the main character.

When I was a teenager, I clairvoyantly saw my first job being at a record store. This was during a time when they existed on a grand scale. They were as big as computers came to be. Out in the distance I saw a clairvoyant moving image of me getting into the film business, working with a popular actress, and eventually writing books as I moved into my 30's and beyond. All of this took place as I saw in the timeline ahead of me.

Sometimes I receive clairvoyant visions while experiencing a lucid dream sequence. This was the case during one circumstance where my Spirit team delivered a particular message to me when I was in a deep sleep. In this instance, they were showing me what many around the world were going through at that particular time, which were an enormous amount of love relationship break ups.

In the dream, my Spirit team guided me through my Third Eye on what I was intended to see. They took me down into what might appear to be a nightmare to the average person. I can handle most anything and am used to some of the abrupt ways delivered messages reach me. It was nighttime when I walked into what appeared to be my house only to find a man standing there facing me. I wondered why he was in my house. He approached me taking a few steps and asked for money. I immediately said, "Sure." I reached into my pocket, but then he rapidly moved towards me in a threatening way. I rose into a panic, "What are you doing?"

Before anything else could happen, he pulled out a switch blade and stabbed me in the heart with enormous force. I felt a huge sharp pain as if it was happening in real time and I was dying. The piercing of the stab in my heart was pulling me deeper into the other world that it felt as if I was experiencing a painful human death. My eyes shot open back on the Earth plane on my bed in the middle of the night and I realized it was no longer happening and I was fine. I collected myself and then brushed it off knowing it was a Divine clairvoyant message. I knew *(claircognizance)* my Spirit team would reveal additional information to the stabbing image when I would fall back asleep again for part two.

I fell into another deep sleep not long afterwards to allow my Spirit team to give me the rest of the message. I heard *(clairaudience)* a loud eerie banging like construction echo going on for several minutes before it stopped. I got up from my bed to investigate and noticed the clock said 3:00 am. I wandered through the house in the dark. I wasn't awake as this was all part of the dream, which didn't feel like a dream as it was occurring. It felt as if I were wide awake and it was happening in real time waking hours. I wandered the halls in the house and slowed down my walk stunned and concerned at what was revealed through my point of view. The tiling from the walls were broken and crumbled all over the floor as if someone took a hammer and went crazy on it. I could see the pipes within the walls. I continued wandering through the house and saw pieces of the plaster on the floor in other rooms. I glazed over it confused and perplexed. Mind you, it was happening as if it were real time as it was incredibly vivid. There was no comprehension that it was a dream.

My eyes shot open with a gasp inhaled in real time as I woke up to notice everything was fine again. I knew then that it never happened. When I looked over I noticed the clock said 3:00 am. Not only was that the time in the dream, but it was the time upon waking. I checked through the house and there was no tiling or plaster on the floor.

I did not have to ask my Spirit team for more clarification because I understood their language and message. They filtered the meaning through claircognizance. The stabbing in my heart by the home invader was telling me that it was to deliver the message that many around the world are experiencing heartache in breakups of all kinds. This was backed up by the abundant amount of messages from readers, friends, and acquaintances I was receiving in my personal life at that time. They were all experiencing a hard relationship break up one on top of the other and all at the same time. It was at an unusually high rate.

The deterioration and crumbling of the walls in my home in the darkness were telling me that these breakups were significantly painful and happening out of nowhere. The darkness in the house points to the heavy grieving they all felt. Those who were experiencing these break ups and endings were feeling as if their whole world was crumbling down. These were not easy breakups taking place in these people's lives. The structure and stability they had come to understand was falling apart. There was much heartbreak within the dynamic of many of the connections. This was no surprise to me because at the time we were also in the midst of the Venus Retrograde planetary transit. This causes relationships or connections that are strained to break apart abruptly and permanently.

Many paranormal connections or disturbances tend to rise during the night. In truth, the larger reason has more to do with the stillness that exists at nighttime. During the day, there is more physical activity and distractions taking place, which prevents one from picking up on spirit paranormal activity. During the night, all of this activity tends to relax and the distractions lesson revealing what is unseen. This is also why many tend to grow more depressed at night after a break up or loss of some kind. You're left in the still quietness, with a hyper focus on your thoughts and feelings. The flipside is if you're doing fine, then at night the messages and guidance can come in more effortlessly.

Those who live in the middle of nowhere, work from home, or have less physical or human distractions in their life will notice an equal amount of spirit activity during the day as they do at night.

In the clairvoyant dream example, you'll notice how you have to become a bit of a detective when translating a message that comes in through the Third Eye.

In another incident, I was in a deep sleep within another vivid Clairvoyant dream as if it was happening in real time. There was a nasty dark ugly poltergeist throwing things at me. Sometimes it would miss me and other times it would fly at me. I'd fend off its repeated attacks by crossing my arms to form an X up in front of me to break the impact, but it was exhausting as this wasn't stopping this thing. Darker entities are threatened by beings that have a brighter lighter around them. This is also apparent on the Earth plane where there are people who permanently reside in the darkness of ego. They are threatened, jealous, and envious of someone with a brighter light. They will attack that person in some manner even if it's through a comment or statement initiated by hiding behind the safety of their computer screen where the person on the receiving end cannot attack them back.

Poltergeist is another name for a noisy ghost or spirit. They are not as bad as Hollywood horror films like to portray them to be. These spirits do not realize what they are doing. They are stuck in a limbo atmosphere without a strong running consciousness. The limbo atmosphere is slightly darker than the Earth plane, and it is no place for any soul to inhabit. It is cold, dark, empty, and desolate. This is felt permanently on all levels until the spirit comes to consciousness and is pleasantly released by moving swiftly into the light.

This poltergeist in the dream was intense due to its real nature and by infiltrating itself into my dream. It's attacks were non-stop causing me exhaustion in the dream. My heart fell into my stomach and I shouted in the dream, "Archangel Michael!" A huge boom sound rang out loudly like a native drum. My surroundings flushed up with super bright light that I couldn't see. It enveloped me while snapping the poltergeist out into oblivion. My eyes shot open as I caught my breath in a gasp again to find myself laying on my bed in real time. An overwhelming feeling of love suddenly enveloped me and took over my soul.

Someone with clairvoyant tendencies will usually have lucid or vivid dreams which evaporate immediately upon wakening. Sometimes this is due to the use of drugs and alcohol. The effects of drugs and alcohol interrupt ones sleep cycle and diminish the amount of REM *(deep dream state)* input. This can cause you to forget your dreams upon waking. When you release the need to consume drugs and alcohol, your body will go through an automatic detox. The detox process is not smooth as inner feelings are coming out of you and your body moves back into re-alignment. When you are no longer on negative substances, your dreams become more lucid. Your consciousness travels out of your body during your dream state. When you go through withdrawals or a detox, then this can lead you to experience fear in your dreams. This is still the case even months after the elimination process associated with a detox. Your subconscious mind and lower self are in a tug of war while in the sleep state.

The use of alcohol and drugs hinder the brain chemicals that transmit messages. When you no longer consume heavy amounts of negative substances, then your brain's neurotransmitters go through a process of re-alignment. Part of this causes an out of body experience. Some will experience flying dreams as well as dream situations surrounding fear. Your soul is not grounded in the physical world. This can assist you in delving deeper into working with methodologies of healing and working with your clairvoyance. Remembering your dreams and having repetitive out of body experiences are signs that your third eye and clairvoyance have opened up or are in the process of opening.

When you notice violet light around the third eye area or in your peripheral vision, then this is a sign that your clairvoyance is opening up or has been activated. Some may choose to hold a quartz crystal point over the Third Eye area for a few minutes or more with the intention of triggering this channel. Sit down or lie down and close your eyes. Keep your physical eyes closed while having the intention that your Third Eye is opening up. Don't force anything to happen, but simply let it be, let it go, and let it flow. Visualize your Third Eye being cracked open. The more you practice to see out of your Third Eye, then the stronger it gets.

Chapter Three

CLAIRAUDIENCE

Clairaudience means *clear hearing* or *clear audio*. Having clairaudience is hearing the voice of God, Spirit, and any being in Heaven. You are hearing the voices of Heavenly messages and guidance being filtered through your etheric ears, located behind your physical ears. The voices can be heard inside or outside your head. This is not to be confused with your own inner voice, which at times can be interchangeable between your voice and Spirits voice.

Your inner voice can be a combination of the voice of Spirit, your higher self, your lower self, and your ego. This is why it can be complicated for those having difficulty deciphering if the voice they hear is their own voice or their Spirit team's.

The obvious way to detect what is your voice or that of any high vibrational spirit is by what ends up coming true in the end. Another rule is that the voice of God or a higher being will never instruct you to hurt, harm, or hate yourself, or another soul at all ever. That is the voice of the lower self and the ego. This means those people who have killed their children, someone else, or a love partner and said God told them to were hearing the voice of their ego and lower self. Some may even be diagnosed with schizophrenia, but have dove into spiritual concepts, which to some extent can be dangerous. The reason is I've witnessed them only focus on the psychic aspects of spiritually based pursuits and have used that as validation and confirmation of the voices they are hearing. Some spiritual concepts are helpful and not harmful, such as prayer and meditation, but they're only excitedly focusing on the psychic bits.

This also means that a terrorist who kills in the name of God is also killing due to the instructions given by their own ego or the ego of another, such as a false prophet. A high vibrational being will never instruct someone to take it upon themselves to hate, hurt, or harm another living soul no matter what they've done. It is not a human being's authority to decide on another's fate.

The voices of spirit are uplifting and calm, even if it is warning you of danger. They will guide, inspire, and lovingly coax you onward on your path. It will warn you of danger or offer words about your life or another that later ends up coming to fruition.

For as long as I can remember, I have heard voices from the spirit world predominately behind one of my physical ears as guidance, information, and messages. The voices of my Guides and Angels are clear as if they are standing next to me talking into an ear that has been deafer than the other since birth.

When I was four years old, my Mother had repeatedly taken me to the Doctor for hearing checkups and tests. They had concern connected to my physical hearing. She later informed me that I was not responding to any of the tests in one of my ears. Therefore, they thought I might be fully deaf in that ear. The sounds of the outside world are fainter in that ear than the other. Instead the volume is cranked up to the spirit world in the deafer ear.

Every now and then I hear a ringing in my ear that has been undetected by medical professionals to be anything of concern. The ringing or buzzing sound is my Spirit team downloading important or vital information that I would need to access at some point. This is a common occurrence when one's clairaudience is calibrating. I equate it to hooking up a flash drive to your computer and moving important files off it and onto your hard drive for immediate access. My Spirit team is transferring and downloading data into my consciousness to be used at a later date. It includes messages, guidance, and information.

At times through clairaudience, I will hear a dial up internet sound in my inner ear when my higher self's consciousness is attempting to connect with Spirit. Other times if the reception is not clear, it will sound as if I am switching the channels on a radio station until I hear a clear song. This is why sometimes I will hear them loud and clear, while other times it will be low and far away if I'm distracted by physical influences. In other words, I'm temporarily blocked as all are in varying degrees throughout each day while living on the physical plane.

Music is and has always been my escape. I love music as I am a rocker after all with those childhood dreams of rocking out on a guitar, but music is the only area I prefer it loud. I could live without communicating in any form except through the sounds of music. As a clairaudient, I hear the heavenly inspiration and messages carried on the notes of music. I hear the words clearly from my Spirit team as I'm listening to the notes and chord changes in a song. The words of Spirit flow and interweave through these notes effortlessly. All other loud sounds and noises are intrusive, strictly shunned, and forbidden around me. This includes sounds such as crowd noise, sirens, airplanes, trashcans banging, screaming of any kind, and traffic echoes. The unpleasant noises are incredibly heightened and uncomfortable.

Many clairaudients can be sensitive to sounds, but at the same time they welcome certain sounds. One of the ways to awakening clairaudience is to pay attention to every sound in your vicinity from a clock ticking, to the roar of an engine in the distance, to a crow squawking, and the birds chirping in the morning. It reminds me of the Jack Nicholson character in the film, "Wolf". Long after he's been bitten by a wolf, he is slowly transitioning into having the qualities of a wolf.

There is a scene where he is at work as an editor at a book publishing company. He rises from his chair in his office and heads out into the main foyer area. His eyebrows are expressive and at attention as he's listening to sounds he had never heard before. There is a close up on his ear hearing every sound at an incredibly high decibel. These include conversations people are having in their offices with the doors closed. He is able to hear those sounds. It sounds almost chaotic, but he is able to bring certain sounds to the forefront, and then push it away to pull another sound up. This is a good depiction of what it is often like for me as a clairaudient. Shuttering at every sound nuance coming in from the spirit world and interrupting or overlapping the sounds in the Earthly physical world.

As a clairaudient, I need white noise playing in the background as it helps to adjust the frequencies in my brain waves. This is the area connected to your clairaudience channel. The algorithms move up and down giving me crystal clear reception to horrible reception. Not only do I need some kind of white noise in the background at all times, but nine times out of ten there is some kind of music playing from the moment I get up and all throughout the day. Sure there are moments of complete silence especially while communing in nature.

The music I play can be any kind of genre of music. If it's not rock, classic rock, or chill-out, then it's ambient sounds. I may have ambient sounds playing in the background as well too, such as sounds in space, in the ocean, the forest, or of heavy winds playing for hours. There are times I've had many things playing in an overlap of symphonic sounds. You walk into one room to find something playing, but you walk into another room to find something else playing. There are also times that I have an ear piece playing music in one ear, while the other ear is left open to hear another sound in the room with me. While this could be distracting for the average person, for me it's soothing as the waves, frequencies, and algorithms are adjusted in my consciousness for clearer spirit reception. It also distracts and greatly diminishes the sounds happening in the physical world, which are mostly made up of unnecessary noise anyway. This doesn't include nature sounds such as the birds singing to the ocean waves crashing.

As an exercise, I pay attention to the physical sounds around me first, then I diminish those sounds in order to hear the sounds from the spirit world rush up.

I hear footsteps around me or someone approaching and I immediately know who is coming, what personality type they are, or if they are a stranger or not. When they appear in my eye line, it turns out to be exactly who I picked up on. I figured I was odd in that I constantly fixated on what others deemed to be an unimportant trivial sound. All sounds are heightened affecting me in ways that it doesn't affect the average person, but may affect someone with clairaudience or one who is sensitive to sounds. Physical world noises and sounds are chaotic and toxic to me. They create a block preventing the higher vibrational sounds from coming in.

I put my inner spark and passion into my writing projects. I hear the rhythms in the music in what's playing around me on the speakers and that is one way that my Spirit team communicates with me. I hear their words in the notes, in the music, in people's conversations, in the line at the store, and it inspires me. I learned over time how to naturally dim the outside sounds in order to hear the Spirit world sounds.

While at the beach, I tap into the sounds of the ocean waves crashing, and the spirit voices rush over that and through this glorious white noise. The music I play translates into verbal messages coming through the sounds and inspiration. It is my own private sonata hearing what someone else might not notice. I hear everything in all sounds, from people's voices, to the patterns in people's footsteps. I can tell what others are up to from those sounds. As a child, I used to think I was a spaz having an acute hearing ability to every sound that happened around me like an alert wild animal who may take fight or flight at any instance. I did not know until adulthood that there was an actual word for it called *clairaudience*. This is because vocabulary and labels are designed by humankind, whereas in the spirit world what exists just is. There is no need to label anything as all souls are created and treated equally.

I've forever heard the voices of Spirit since I was a kid. It was never unusual and has perpetually been a part of my everyday life for as long as I can remember. I was having conversations with those I could not see. Sometimes members of my Spirit team speak individually and other times it's in unison or harmony. The voices are slightly different from my own voice, although occasionally it might even sound like my own voice coming in from an alternate Universe. Growing up, I also did not know there was a name for it. It's not like this is studied in schools growing up, although spiritual studies should be a big part of the education system. It is non-denominational and helps in empowering and inspiring every individual. It would definitely assist in altering the world for the better by teaching others class etiquette. There would be less negativity and hostile ego bullying, with more love and joy on Earth being exuded.

Little did I know that these guides were a Spirit team or that they were living in a place that some call Heaven. There was no label for who they are or where they are. I had never thought much about where they live, or where they were communicating with me from. It's not like one day I woke up and there they were around me. When anyone grows from birth, to baby, to toddler, you gradually become aware of your surroundings. This is how it was for me. What I did know without question was they were/are like family and have my greatest interests at heart. I knew/know their intention was to not only watch over me, but work with me. There has never been any kind of condescending attitudes while working with them. It's never felt as if they owned me or anything like that. I've known they were on my level working with me, and helping in areas that are out of my hands in the physical world. I also knew as a child that they were not on the Earth plane. It didn't occur to me at the time to ask where they were talking to me from, because it was as if I just knew. If all you know is one way of life from the time you're born, then you don't question it since it is all you know. It's kind of like celebrity children who are unaware that their parent or parents are famous to the world as an actor, singer, etc. Children of celebrities are not conscious or caring about any of that. They only know the parent to just be mom or dad. They don't know any differently. This is the same way it was with my Spirit team growing up. I didn't know any other way of life because they've forever been around communicating with me for as long as I can remember.

One afternoon I was running late to an appointment and I could not find my car keys anywhere. I started throwing everything around in a panic mentally shouting, "Where are my keys!"

I huffed and puffed throwing items all over the place in a panic. I shouted again, "Angels! Where are my keys?!"

I heard a loud male voice in my left ear shout, "On your bed!!" Without hesitating, I charged into the bedroom. There were my keys on the bed sitting all alone. I grabbed them abruptly and headed towards my car. I mentally repeated the words to my Spirit team, "Thank you. Thank you. Thank you."

Heaven is unfazed by your sudden upset. All they see is the love buried inside you. This does not give one license to behave as I did, but as you work with them more, you are less hostile and more appreciative. They see the light within you and ignore the range of wasted emotions, because to them everything is all right. In that instance, I called my team, "Angels", but what I call them varies from time to time. In the end, it doesn't matter as they know I'm addressing them regardless of what I choose to call them as a group.

As my interest in the spiritually based crowd grew, I wanted to know what those in that group were like since I never believed I fit into any group. While I still do not believe or see me as fitting into any group, I have a stronger appreciation and love for the spiritual community. I have made an endless amount of loving friendships with so many in those communities as well as those who are part of my soul family back home only to connect this lifetime.

One year, I went to an all-day spiritually based convention event to be around like-minded souls. While there, I agreed to give someone a cold reading in the audience for fun. This was not a test, but an exercise using no divination tool such as oracle or tarot cards. I personally did not need them even though part of me enjoyed double-checking and confirming the messages through those tools. This is where the angels reminded me once again as they do repeatedly with all of us, "Trust."

Having to do a cold read in a space with hundreds of people's energies around me while on little sleep was not my cup of tea. I wondered why

I agreed to it as I was mentally preparing and adjusting my frequencies. I wanted to bolt out of there at lightning speed and crawl back into bed. I knew there was no way out now that I agreed, and when I commit to something no matter what it is, I see it through. I could feel my Spirit team pushing me out of my comfort zone. I asked for a volunteer to participate in this exercise.

A young girl who was sitting near me raised her hand and said she will be the willing participant. I had her pull her chair to face me and close her eyes. I reached my hand out around her head to feel the air pressure energy. My Spirit team said that this was not about me. This is about this girl in front of me. I closed my eyes and took several deep breaths until I was relaxed.

I called in my Spirit team and said, "Please get my ego out of the way. This is about this girl right here. It is all about her and not me. If anyone would like to come through for her, please come forward now."

I mentally repeated those words with my eyes closed waiting in stillness for some communication in any form. I heard a male voice speak loud and clear through my clairaudience channel. My ego was naturally trying to make me second-guess it. I opened my eyes and what I said stopped her:

"There is a pleasant man who is around you right now. He says he is always with you. He is telling me that his name is Ralph. He is your grandfather. He has been working closely with you on your education and towards your life purpose."

I noticed the girl's eyes flooded with tears

which stopped me as I wondered why she was so overflowing with emotion. She informed me that she is sixteen years old and in High School. I thought she was in her early twenties as she had a mature look to her. She carried herself confidently as if she were an adult. She was also at this conference alone. She said her Mother's Dad, her Grandfather, died when she was seven years old. She then said that his name was "Ralph".

Most of the time you are getting accurate information and messages from your own Spirit team, but you discredit it or talk yourself out of it being real. I heard a male voice clearly telling me his name for this young girl. I thought I was imagining it at first. I was thinking, "I don't know any Ralph. This is silly."

My Spirit team prompted me to trust in the communication I was getting and not second guess it. It may not mean anything to me, but it might mean something to someone else. I bit the bullet and decided to tell the girl what I heard knowing that I might be wrong. This was an excellent case where I realized again that there are loved ones communicating with you in Heaven. This was a complete stranger whom I had never met, nor had I known anything about her. Yet, I told her about her deceased grandfather.

This is one of the endless examples as to why I've never been an atheist, even though I question everything and I'm skeptical about anything. My entire life has been filled with unexplained psychic related information coming through. I know that the spirit goes somewhere after a human death, because they communicate with me as if they're still very much alive if not more so after they've gone. They also sound completely content, happy, and together. Therefore, I know they're not in a horrid place either.

I am not a working Medium, but what I did in that instance for that girl was what one would call, *Mediumship*. This is something anyone can do if they work at it. Do not doubt or second-guess the messages you receive. Do not worry if you make a mistake. That's already going to be a given and you have nothing to prove to anybody including yourself. Communicating with spirit is a God given gift that all are capable of. When you second guess information then you are operating from your imposter lower self or ego who wants to convince you that you're wrong. You may pick up on information that means nothing to you, but it could mean something to someone else. You also want to use discernment and tread carefully about not approaching someone to offer them psychic information on themselves, unless that person has specifically granted you permission to do so. This conflicts with the free will law in place by God.

All souls are capable of reading for another, but they all read in a variety of different ways. Everyone has the same gifts of clair channel communication, but how those gifts work in the physical world for that soul varies between people. For example, some people will need to have the person in front of them to read them, while others need to have them on the phone to hear their voice vibration, or to pick up on their energy. I do not need to see or hear the person. My sensitivities are too keen to every nuance around me that I have found it to be more of a distraction at times. Due to having clairaudience, I am able to hear the voice of spirit without having the person present. The voices are louder when I'm in a centered state. Sometimes my Spirit team chimes in before someone has finished their sentence!

You can differentiate between the voices of you, and the voices of Heaven by its accuracy of the message being relayed. When you look back during the times you were in danger, you might recall when you received a heavenly message through a clair channel. When there is an urgent situation that could put you in danger, you may hear a voice that urges you to get up and get out of a particular place. You later protest that if you didn't run out of there who knows what might've happened.

Clairaudience is one of my strongest clairs *(next to Claircognizance)*. I hear voices, words, and sounds coming in through one of my ears that later comes true. My Clairaudience has been one of the main convincers for me throughout the course of my life that has made me a believer of another world beyond this one. This is because of the content of the voices and words that have been relayed to me. My Spirit team has uttered names, phrases, and words from someone who has long passed on to the other side. That is one of the greatest convincers for me especially when the information has been about a stranger whom I know nothing about.

From an early age, it made me a believer in

knowing that people don't actually die. Because those that have passed on are talking to me from somewhere else. I can hear them and they sound great! The other stuff are the words and phrases my Spirit team has relayed to me on a day to day basis that ends up coming true in my own life. They are communicating to me from somewhere. It's not some dark black void, because they are cheerful, content, strong, and loving. They are doing incredible, so I know they're happy wherever they are. This is what has made me a believer in an afterlife from an early age.

Hearing things about others or that can assist me in my own life through the Clairaudience channel is what has convinced me that there is more to this life than this plane. Deceased loved ones are not dead in the sense that one believes someone to be dead. They reside 'somewhere' and are alive and well. Having these occurrences happen sporadically throughout my life since I was old enough to construct sentences has convinced me that this is not the end. I may not be able to hand over the material physical concrete proof that a non-believing atheist would desire, but I have proof enough for myself. And when you tune into the vibrations around you, then you start to notice the synchronicities that seem beyond physical control that make you a believer too.

Whether someone believes in an afterlife or not is their journey to face, while I have mine. I would not and could not force feed anything to anyone that does not have some measure of truth to it for me. This means I also do not blindly follow what I'm being told or hear. I need to have some kind of evidence that convinces me personally. I cannot fake something and I certainly wouldn't know how to fake something like this anyway, nor would I have an interest in doing so.

Those with higher ranges of clairaudience tend to be musicians, singers, and all those who work with sounds on some level throughout their life. They might not be aware they have clairaudience, but they can certainly develop it. If someone's work is connected to sounds and music, then they hear guidance and messages through the notes of these sounds. Ludwig Van Beethoven composed some of the most memorable and beloved music in history, yet he was also considered deaf. This irony begged others to question, "How on Earth did he write these incredible pieces if he is deaf?"

His hearing was faint, but spirit infused his clairaudience channel with music that has long been remembered over the centuries. Hearing the music through clairaudience for a piece of music that a songwriter writes points to having a strong Divine connection. Many musicians have this gift without realizing it. Some may not know that the inspiration and gifts are coming from above, while others acknowledge some measure of cosmic power filtering into them.

Other clairaudients may find that they mumble or talk to themselves, and yet they're perfectly sane. They find they're having conversations with spirit without realizing it or trying to. It's talking to them as if you talk to a friend on the phone. The conversations or talking isn't random and full of gibberish. It is clear concise information that later proves to be true, or is positively helpful to that person or another. This also takes us to the days back in history when humankind would punish or lock up someone who heard voices or talked to themselves. Humankind would also put the person on medication to quiet the voices. It is true some people are genuinely not receiving clairaudient messages from spirit, and instead are hearing voices that come from their ego or the result of being on medication or intoxicated, but there are also a number of people who are communicating genuine Divine messages from above.

The singer Stacy Ferguson, also known as Fergie from the band The Black Eyed Peas, had once battled an addiction to crystal methamphetamine for nearly a year. She has openly talked about that period in her life and in hearing voices that she believed to be legitimate. These voices were convincing her of negative circumstances such as the FBI being after her. While in the throes of the addiction she escaped to hide out in a church fearing she was being followed. While in the church, her angels intervened and more or less said, "Okay, go outside and if there is no one out there chasing after you, then this is your confirmation that these conspiracies are drug related and have nothing to do with God. If there is no one out there waiting for you, then you will quit using this drug."

To make a long story short, she went outside and found no one out there. She had that epiphany moment realizing, "Wow, this has all been in my head." She soon began the work to dissolve the addiction to the drug.

You can understand by this example that some of the voices Fergie heard were her own ego and chemical drug induced, but then they were also genuine when it intervened and made a deal to prove her conspiracy paranoia was coming from the voice of her ego.

Heaven instructs or offers messages and guidance that can help that individual or another person positively with compassion. Those who are clairaudient will hear things that no one else can hear.

Tanya, a Mother in Washington, was folding laundry near her baby. It wasn't any different than any other day, except this time she couldn't shake this foreboding feeling that kept overcoming her. It was growing to the point where she heard a loud voice through clairaudience shout, "Run!"

She wasn't a big believer of anything and nor was she spiritual, but this shook her to the core. She grabbed her baby and left the room abruptly. As that happened, she heard the loud sounds of a tree falling. She turned around to see what had just happened and discovered this tree had collapsed into her house on the spot she was standing minutes before with her child. She not only picked up Heavenly guidance, but she paid attention to it and took action. This saved both she and her child's life, or at least prevented major injury. This made her consider the possibility that she may not be moving through life alone and is indeed watched over by a Heavenly team.

Do not discredit the guidance and messages that are being filtered through you by your Spirit team on a regular basis. Some of the guidance might seem insignificant or subtle causing you to brush it off, but could ultimately be a life saver as illustrated.

I'm a lifelong beach bum having lived in coastal cities for more than half my life. However, I did temporarily move myself out of my element and at the foot of the Hollywood Hills for three years. When it was time for me to move back to the beach, I called upon my Spirit team to assist. It was about six weeks of looking at places when I came down to two runner ups. There were two places I liked, but I was on the fence as to which would be best for me in the end. While riding down in an elevator in a high rise corporate business building, a nice sociable woman entered the elevator and chatted me up. For some reason she weaved into her sentence that she lived in "Beach Cities" (we'll call it), even though I didn't ask. I never saw her again after that. The next day as I was entering another building, a group of men were walking together and talking over one another as they were exiting the building. I heard one of the men say to another as I passed them, "Yeah, it's in Beach Cities." I overheard just enough of the conversation to note the forecast of where I was going to ultimately be moving to next.

What is interesting is that is the place I ultimately ended up moving to as the other place fell apart. This is an example of how clairaudience can come about through audible words by someone else saying just what you needed to hear. There was no reason for this woman or man to be bringing up "Beach Cities", especially since no one talks about that city. I have also never heard anyone ever utter that city again since. I heard just enough of the conversation to pick up on the psychic forecast that my Spirit team was trying to relay to me when I needed an answer. Clairaudience comes in the form of other people's words containing the answer you need to hear.

Other forms of clairaudience are hearing your voice being spoken to you. When I had entered my teen years I was riding a skateboard and could hear a disembodied voice saying my name repeatedly through one of my ears. The voice warned me to be careful. I did a pop-a-wheelie and slammed down off the curb and came crashing down to the floor breaking my two front teeth. No one would be able to detect it today as the dentistry field is pretty miraculous able to create a look-a-like replacement that was even better than what was there before, but it wasn't without hours of endless surgery. Spirit was warning me within about 10-15 minutes before the accident, but I ignored it causing this catastrophic result. Clearly, I don't always follow their guidance, especially not when I was a rebellious punk teen. On some occasions when I've ignored them, I've kicked myself later and said, "You tried to warn me and I refused to listen. I had that coming."

Hearing your guide or angel can be hearing one or two word phrases to long drawn out sentences. Pay attention to the vibrations of your own speaking voice and how you communicate. Also notice the sounds of how other people speak and communicate. This assists in understanding the rhythms of sound, which is connected to clairaudience.

Another incident while driving home one day, I heard my Grandmother talking to me through my clairaudience channel. I was confused for a moment as the voice was disembodied the way my Spirit team's voices and those in Heaven sound to me, and my Grandmother was still alive. When I arrived back home I received a call from a family member that my Grandmother was in the Hospital as she's going into surgery. I was perplexed again because she had just communicated with me in a way that only those on the other side do. Hours later, I discovered from another family member that she had passed away, and that when I was notified of her surgery, she had already passed on, but it was so unexpected that the family member made up a story that she was going into major surgery to delay having to tell anyone she passed all of a sudden.

This scenario also just goes to show you that you can't try and pull a fast one with someone highly connected with spirit on some level, as I thought something was suspiciously off when my Grandmother spoke to me from the other side before I was told of her passing.

Clairaudience is not just through your clear hearing channel, but it can also come through on a song on the radio or a line said in a movie. This is where you hear just enough of it that it triggers a psychic hit prompting you to know for sure that it is a message you are indeed intended to hear.

One morning I awoke and immediately went into a channel with my Guides and Angels. This is common for me as I find it to be a great way to start the day. You are super relaxed and open to communicate. This one particular morning when I awoke, my team asked me to turn the little radio on that sits next to me, which I never do. I reached over and hit the "on" switch near my bed.

The first few chords of the next classic rock song began called, "Spirit in the Sky". I thought that was incredibly fitting and pretty humorous that I turned it on at just the right chord. Those in Heaven have great laughter and senses of humor. This is why they urge you to have the same. They prepared me for the day and to remember that we're never alone. Your Guides and Angels around you communicate to you in various ways and sometimes through music! This was their way of telling me they enjoyed connecting if only briefly after I woke up.

Chapter Four

CLAIRCOGNIZANCE

Claircognizance means *clear knowing* or *clear awareness*. Heavenly messages and guidance falls through your consciousness from above in the form of thoughts, words, or ideas. It is having crystal clear perception or knowing the answer to a topic or subject matter that you are not typically versed in.

Many of the world's mature thinkers, communicators, and inventors tend to have claircognizance as their primary dominate clair. This is where you suddenly receive a bright idea or a flash of clarity where you know what you're intended to do or say in a situation that ends up assisting you or another in a positive way. You're sitting around stumped trying to find an answer to something, but then suddenly you receive a flash of brilliant awareness energy where the answer or guidance appears to you out of nowhere. You call out, "I've got it!" Others wonder where you received this answer from as you were just sitting there when the answer appeared and jolted you into excitement. This is an example of claircognizance.

One of my dominate clairs is clairaudience, but the other dominate clair is claircognizance. Like the beings I describe in my book, *Realm of the Wise One*, those guys on the other side tend to have claircognizance as a dominate clair trait while living an Earthly life. The mind of a claircognizant is like its own private working computer that seems to sift and find information it needs that can help you or another positively. You receive Divine information, messages, and guidance that falls from above and into your mind that later proves to be true.

Those with claircognizance are the thinkers of the world who bring positive change that can help move humanity and the planet forward. Many of them take on life purpose job roles such as inventors, scientists, teachers, counselors, problem solvers, speakers, research investigators, and writers. It is not uncommon for someone with claircognizance to be a non-believer of anything beyond the human physical life. They might not believe in God or an afterlife for that matter. They need concrete evidence before they become a believer, but even then they still function with some measure of uncertainty while requiring concrete tangible proof.

Wise Ones operate primarily through claircognizance where the answers to questions they're not versed in seem to fall into their consciousness naturally. Like the claircognizant, a Wise One will rarely go to someone else for answers, wisdom, messages, or assistance, because the Wise One is the chap who is approached for that knowledge. Claircognizants seem to know the right answer to most anything, or they know what to say to others that can help them.

Since I was child I have had others pose the same repeated question at one time or another, "How did you know that was going to happen?" or "You're right. How did you know that?"

In the earlier days, I'd grow perplexed not knowing, "I don't know. I just knew."

I did not know how I knew something, but the answer seemed to fall into me from above. Those who operate purely from an analytical or scientific level first before anything else usually have claircognizance as their stronger clair.

Signs of claircognizance is knowing the right answer to something where there is no way you could know. It comes to you from out of nowhere. Someone with claircognizance also seems to know when someone is lying to them, even if they don't call them out on it. You won't be able to pull a fast one with someone operating with strong claircognizance.

In the past, when I've known someone is lying, I would typically keep it to myself unless it is something major that needs addressing. This information proves useful on occasion, but then there are certain things you do not want to know and would prefer to be naïve to. You know this information is passed onto you for a reason. It is to protect you or someone else by saving them time and potential heartache. This can be someone you like romantically. You suspect they have ulterior motives with you, and this later ends up coming true. This suspicion that comes in the form of thoughts or is suddenly present in your mind feels like an energized jolt that awakens you to this knowledge.

A claircognizant would know if someone is betraying them or someone else too. I have known things about someone from a first meeting and what they are like, what to be weary of, and what to pay attention to. I can tell immediately what role they would play in my life if any. Everyone I dated romantically, I knew at first glance that I would be with them soon or in the future. It would later happen and come to fruition. There was no explanation for it and I never questioned it. This is an example of what claircognizance and clear knowing is. You won't second guess claircognizance, because the sense of knowing is extremely powerful where you know without a doubt what the answer, guidance, or message is.

Psychic information, messages, or guidance in general comes to you when you are not trying to get it. When you push to receive guidance or messages, then that is when you block it. Your fear is that you will not pick up on any messages, or that the messages you receive are your imagination. As a result, you hear and receive nothing. When you second guess what you're receiving, then that creates a block.

Your Spirit team is continually communicating

with you, but your strong will to try to receive messages can dim the connection causing you to pick up on nothing. The underlying core reason is due to fear, or destructive and unhelpful self-talk. Negative emotions block communication with the other side. You can call on your Spirit team to remove the blocks that cut off the communication to them. Ask to help you clearly hear, see, know, and feel the messages they wish to relay to you.

One Summer, I was talking with a group of people standing in a circle at a beach BBQ. There were many huddles of people talking at this BBQ around my group too. As I was talking to them, I took one-step back grabbing the bottle of wine behind me to my right. I proceeded to pour it into the glass of a woman who was in another huddle near my group. She jolted in shock and laughed into a shout. "I was just going to get more wine! Wait! How did you know that? Okay, that was weird."

I shrugged and said, "I don't know. I just knew." I had no idea how I knew and I was not looking at the woman or facing her. I was busy talking to someone in my own group. Something had prompted me to turn, grab the wine, and pour without questioning it. Sometimes the clear knowing is slight and can surround something as insignificant as this. You are just highly aware and in tune to your surroundings to the point that your reflex is to go with it.

Other examples of having claircognizance are where you know the answers to problems or topics you are not educated in, yet you had the right answer that solved it when others were perplexed. People with an analytical mind such as a Scientist or Teacher are great problem solvers, which points to claircognizance capabilities. Their Spirit team filters this information through them.

Ironically, those with claircognizance tend to also be the ones who are skeptical of psychic phenomena. They are left brained people who function primarily through logic. They might not necessarily be a believer of a higher power or an afterlife, even if they are receiving Divine guidance. One of the reasons is due to their analytical or scientific mind. They need concrete proof of anything unseen with their physical eyes. Yet, they're receiving heavenly guidance through their claircognizance channel regardless. Psychic phenomena is not reserved to the believers. In fact, many non-believers may reveal to have these unexplainable psychic premonitions over someone who is a believer. The reason is because they're not trying to connect to a higher power and therefore are facing no roadblocks or resistance. They're just living life going through the motions and this guidance is falling through their consciousness. It's happening naturally even if they pull back to say, "Wow, not sure how I came up with this. It just came to me."

It may take some of them awhile to put it together that there must be some cosmic force at play. It doesn't occur to them that it was filtering through them from above. They shun anything connected to psychic phenomena not truly understanding what that entails. They are unaware that they are indeed psychic! Whereas a believer is trying with all their might to receive something and therefore receives nothing. It's the trying to receive an answer that pushes the answer away.

Many that have come across me over the course of my life would comment that I am wise beyond my years. As I've grown older, it's not terribly unusual to be known as wise, but this wise comment goes back to childhood. In High School, I was the guy who would sit up in the bleachers and one by one a different student would approach me to divulge their issues as if I were their own private counselor. They were from every different clique and label you could imagine. The nerd, the jock, the cheerleader, the techie, the bully, and the bullied would all come up to me solo at varying intervals. I would say a sentence or two to them that assisted their situation. They would cry out in relief with something along the lines of, "God, you always know just what to say!"

Some of them would say things like, "It's as if you're this old soul who knows the answers to life and yet you're a teenager in High School. It's kind of cool. How do you know so much?"

At the time, it hadn't occurred to me where this information was coming from. It took me awhile to realize, "Oh, this is coming from my Spirit team."

In those days growing up, the Internet, computers, and cell phones had not yet taken off. If someone had a computer, they were considered well to do and of higher means financially. It wasn't common to have gadgets like that yet. DVD players didn't exist and we were still playing VHS cassette tapes. I also didn't read much as I have ADD/ADHD and have trouble retaining any information as it is. This makes reading challenging, but not entirely impossible. I have to constantly re-read a line as I've forgotten it after I've read it. If someone lectures for longer than fifteen minutes, then they've lost me no matter how interesting the topic is. For that matter, there is no doubt that all of the books I've written have indeed been divinely guided since that is the only area where focus seems to be present. This is an example of claircognizance in action. It's the one area where having patient disciplined focus exists. I am cruising through a channel euphoric high while creating.

The claircognizance channel can be one of the more difficult channels to connect with for others because you're not receiving psychic visuals (clairvoyance), or hearing it (clairaudience), or feeling it (clairsentience). You learn to realize that you 'know' it without a doubt. There is no emotion with claircognizance, which is why many who primarily use that clair may come off cold, detached, aloof, or unemotional to anything. For that matter, they can make great leaders because their emotions don't get the best of them and rarely grow unstable. They function calmly and rationally.

I knew I was different growing up, but the majority around me seemed to appreciate this eccentricity, which is unusual considering the darkness of ego in others threatened by the unconventional. There were no cell phones when I was growing up, and so the majority of interaction with others took place in person face to face. You developed highly keen social skills, which translates to a higher mental capacity. This mental capacity is greasing the wheels to a finely calibrated claircognizant channel. Someone gets to know you and a soul connection is easily made. It keeps you witty and on your toes. Whereas today most everyone hides behind a computer system or technological gadget, which masks the disconnected unhappy distance inside.

I was walking past a colleague from a former job. He said, "Hey Kevin, I want to ask you a question. What do you think of bacon toothpaste?"

Without flinching or displaying shock I immediately said, "I don't know. That sounds like something someone in Iowa would invent."

His face flushed in shock. "How the Hell did you know that?"

I stood in silence stumped for a second, "I don't know."

He proceeds to inform me while pointing to the chat box on his computer screen, "I'm talking to a friend of mine online who is in Iowa and he was just telling me that he's working on inventing this toothpaste with bacon in it. Okay, Kevin that was weird. How did you know that?"

"I - I don't know. It's just what I thought of."

This is another example of claircognizance in action where you know the accurate answers and do not know how you know. Not long afterwards, I overheard him telling someone of our exchange. He was fascinated that I blurted out an answer that no one ever would have said....unless they were observing a high degree of claircognizance.

Because this is a regular occurrence for me, I never found it to be appropriate to get into a lengthy explanation with anyone about it. There is no efficient way of explaining how a claircognizant knows something. It appears as if you grabbed it out of thin air. I ignore the question or run over it with something else. As a Claircognizant, I know just how to respond.

Someone with claircognizance will receive messages and guidance from Heaven being dropped into their mind. They will typically announce something that they have no way of knowing only to find that it later comes true. When asked how they know this information, they will be unable to efficiently answer the question. They have no idea how they came to receive this sudden insight. The messages sift into them out of nowhere. Someone will say, "You're absolutely right! How did you know that?" You'll look at them stunned and say, "I don't know. It just came to me."

When someone exhibits claircognizance, they have the presence of someone in control and in command. They seem to have the answer for anything and everything that ends up assisting others in a positive way. Their mind is constantly turned on. It appears to be in motion as they continue to make mental lists that periodically come to them throughout each day. When you receive a lightning bolt idea out of the blue that brings you success, then you can be assured that your claircognizant channel is functioning in top form.

Perhaps you're driving through a new town with a friend only to discover that you're both lost. You ask for heavenly assistance and then blurt out, "Turn left up ahead." When you turn left, you both find that you're no longer lost and know where you are. This is an example of receiving assistance through your claircognizant channel.

On another scale, someone with deep claircognizance would be someone like Alexander Graham Bell's connection with the invention of the telephone or Thomas Edison and electricity. They received Divine information that guided them to these inventions in order to progress human life forward with the practical necessities to help them survive more readily. Writers tend to use a good deal of claircognizance as they channel the words from above and onto the page.

Claircognizance is knowing what's coming up ahead or how something works without being versed in it. The information sifts into your consciousness from seemingly out of nowhere. This later proves true or it is positively helpful to you or someone else.

Someone with claircognizance has a tendency to tune everyone out unless it's a super important bullet point. They're the ones that interrupt others while in a conversation to bring their expertise or examples to what someone is talking about. They cannot help it as the information, guidance, and messages flow effortlessly and quickly through the individual's claircognizance channel in an excited rush. This isn't to be confused with someone who interrupts others repeatedly for the sake of attention and to hear themselves talk, although many claircognizant people may do that. The messages the claircognizant picks up have an underlying tone of excitement. Suddenly the messenger cannot control themselves and need to share it immediately.

My mind is constantly on, thinking, analyzing, and working. Sometimes I find it difficult to shut it off when I need it to. I had asked my Doctor once if there was a pill I could take that would help me to stop thinking specifically at night when the thoughts pointlessly move into overdrive. He laughed and said, "Unfortunately, there isn't anything like that."

It was something that I had to accept as a gift and learn to use to my advantage. Knowing things before they happened and not known how or why has saved my life in many great ways. Yet, everyone has access to this sense of knowing.

Someone with claircognizance may have difficulty sleeping as the thoughts in their mind never shut off. This isn't someone who has the occasional restless sleep over an issue that's happening to them personally, nor is it the restless sleep conjured up by a stressful time in your life. Claircognizant people are tossing and turning from birth until human death, even when life is going great. Some of them may be prone to taking a sleeping pill, herbal relaxer, and even something harder at night. Otherwise their mind will never shut off and they'll never sleep.

Claircognizant people are continually thinking causing others to comment that they can see their wheels constantly churning behind their eyes. The claircognizant loves words and communication, whether that is being an avid writer, passionate reader, enthusiastic speaker, or all of the above. While musicians and singers are more apt to having clairaudience, someone with claircognizance would be the songwriter of lyrics. The clairaudient would be the one jotting down the musical notes since they hear the sounds.

Because claircognizant people tend to have the right answers or know what to tell others that can assist that individual, this makes them the go to person whenever someone is having any kind of issue. It is rare for the claircognizant to go to anyone for advice, since they already *know* the answers naturally. If they do go to someone else for an answer, then it's to compare the wisdom or receive another point of view since they are a lifelong teacher/student type. Mostly the claircognizant is a self-sufficient person who relies on no one to thrive or get by. It is beneath them to beg, ask for a hand out, or fall into the superficiality of human practical life. The claircognizant can be seen as a small child as having those abilities if they display problem solving attitudes. They love to build and put toys together while figuring out how something works. They may constantly pepper you with inquisitive questions as they're fascinated by ideas and the inner workings of someone else's mind. In love, they revel in positive words that a lover bestows on them over receiving a practical gift.

Telepathy is another form of claircognizance.

You are receiving telepathic claircognizant hits without realizing it. A telepathic hit example would be when you are thinking of someone you haven't communicated with for a while, and then suddenly they contact you out of the blue to say they were thinking of you and wanted to reach out. You might say to them, "How odd, as I was just thinking about you recently."

Your phone rings and you know exactly who it is before you check it or answer it. You go over to your phone and the telepathic claircognizant hit you received turns out to be true. This seems to be one of the most common claircognizant hits that others have protested to experience, including the non-believers of psychic phenomena.

Your Spirit team plants information into your consciousness for a reason. Maybe it's to remind you of the good that existed in that person and how they made you feel. Perhaps it's to bring you both together again to resolve old issues and bring the connection to proper closure. Or it could be that you or this other person have information or wisdom that is passed onto you when you have that conversation. Sometimes it can simply be a good, positive, fun discussion that uplifts you out of a mood you've been in or it's you who uplifts them.

I receive endless random claircognizant hits on a regular basis, such as seemingly trivial stuff. I know I will hear from a particular person I haven't heard from in a long time. At some point within one to three days, I will receive a text, email, or call from that person. I knew they would be contacting me as that was the psychic hit I previously received.

This is one example of having the psychic sense of knowing.

Telepathy is what is unspoken, but soon proves to be true. It can be that someone is thinking of you and then transmitting this information to you. This alerts you to suddenly be thinking of them. Some say when you're thinking of someone that they are likely thinking of you. While this can certainly be true, typically one of you ends up reaching out to the other at some point not long afterwards. The telepathy has a measure of psychic foresight to it. You both had a telepathic communication line flowing back and forth between your souls. You can also have telepathic communication with a soul on the other side, such as a departed loved one.

Telepathy is similar to claircognizance as it is transmitting thoughts to another person to which they confirm they're receiving. There are certain love relationships or friendships where the two people seem to have a short hand intuiting exactly what the other is saying without words. These are the deep soul mate connections on Earth. The primary way of communication on the other side is through telepathy.

I was on the phone with my mother who was telling me that one of her husband's cat's was not friendly at all. This cat was always hiding somewhere and she could never find him. I closed my eyes and mentally connected to the cat and called to it while my mom spoke about other things. About a few minutes in, my mom stopped talking and started shrieking, "Oh my God! He's coming over to me!? What did you do??"

I connected and communicated to him telepathically and asked him to walk over to her. She said this was the first time she had ever seen this cat do that. This is an example of soul to soul telepathic claircognizant contact. You are doing that often on a regular basis without realizing it.

How many times do you and a close friend finish one another's sentences? Or how many times do you know exactly what someone is going to do? Even though there is no clue that would reveal that. These claircognizant hits sometimes pop up in the most insignificant cases such as where you might know what a car on the road is going to do and then the car does just that seconds later. You receive a psychic hit on knowing when to travel somewhere or when to leave the house. All of these little day to day claircognizant hits help you navigate efficiently through your practical life in the smallest of ways, but in the end are important in that it makes for a smoother ride than if you weren't paying attention to any of it. Test this hypothesis for yourself. This is by following what you're getting, and then on other occasions notice when you opted against it only to find that something doesn't go according to plan as a result.

You can transmit thoughts, words, instructions, or ideas from one claircognizant channel to another. This is essentially what your Spirit team is doing with you. They are communicating with you telepathically, which is the universal communicating method back home in Heaven.

I've transmitted telepathic thoughts to past

lovers or jobs that I wanted only to find that what I transmitted in that direction ended up coming true. In that respect, be careful what you wish for and how you direct your thoughts because you just might get it! Your thoughts are connected to claircognizance, so it's a matter of learning to decipher which thoughts are ego related and which are Divinely guided.

All of the jobs I desired with passion, I would go after them and receive it without hesitance or doubt. I knew (claircognizance) I would get into the film business and that I would one day be an author. There was no negative self-talk and nor did I allow any outside source stop me or say that I can't do that. If there were, then that was fuel to slam on the gas forward to my goal.

I sent out positive thoughts of what I wanted through my claircognizant channel and I would watch it all fall into place and come to fruition at some point. This also means that I've misused my claircognizant channel in the past and brought that which I did not want into my life. You gradually learn to be cognizant of the energy of the thoughts you are having.

One of the big concerns others have posed is wondering if they are on the right path. Having strong claircognizance assists you in becoming more sure of yourself and the path you're on. Those with claircognizance are confident in their answers without fear or worry that they are blurting out the wrong answer or that they're on the wrong path. They receive a random psychic hit and they say it.

Be cognizant, aware, or mindful of something, but it doesn't have to dominate your thoughts. Being cognizant is connected to claircognizance where you know, are aware, or mindful of something. You are alerted to the truth.

I've never questioned the validity of Heaven or that guides and angels exist. While many adults grow jaded to anything unseen, I never did in that respect. This is why connecting has come naturally to me because I'm not second guessing anything. The answer is either there or it's not. The areas I did grow jaded were in the genres of love and relationships, but that's a story for another book. The key to recognizing the presence of your Spirit team is to remove the suspension of disbelief and bring yourself back to that place you had as a child. This is where you had no judgment or criticisms about yourself or others. You were open and receptive to any and all around you. Children have stronger belief systems in place than adults.

False guidance can come about when you are pushing for an answer to come to the point where it feels like you're reaching or randomly guessing. Let go of the need to struggle for an answer and stay centered and receptive. True guidance will come in the form of repetitive hunches to you to take an action on something, even though you keep brushing it off until one day you snap out of that. "Wait a minute, I keep getting that I need to…." You go after the hunch and it ends up positively changing your life.

On the flipside, some have admitted that they thought they were following heavenly guidance only to have it backfire on them. One of the reasons is that you or the other person was operating out of free will. It can also be that the guidance wasn't Divine after all, and was coming from your ego. This is how you learn to differentiate what is and what is not Divinely guided. When one learns how to ride a bike, they might fall off numerous times before finally being able to bike effortlessly.

False guidance has a desperate negative feeling to it. It pushes you to act out recklessly or restlessly. It may also prompt you to act out of character or go after an idea that is far-fetched and out of the ordinary for you. It might be a get rich quick scheme, which are typically questionable endeavors anyway. An unstoppable need to be famous falls into false guidance. This is witnessed more than ever before with many trying to get famous for the sake of being famous, but without actually contributing anything to the arts or to positively move humanity forward in evolving. There are also many talented artists that are famous, but live a quiet life and you never hear about them. Someone can become well known as a result of their creative life purpose work, but their core drive is not for the benefit of being famous. That's merely an added side effect on top of being divinely guided to pursue a particular dream purpose that assists others in some way if even to entertain.

Pay attention to the thoughts that fall into your mind. If the thoughts are abusive or condescending on any level, then that is your lower self and ego. If the thoughts are uplifting and empowering in a way that assists you or another in a positive fashion, then this is Heavenly guidance.

A young man named Robert was bathed in constant insecurities. He would receive irrational abrupt information pushing him to make a decision that ultimately came off dangerous, hasty, and out in left field. These ideas he received either never panned out or they ended up being less than successful. This is because the hits were not divinely guided. The ideas were coming to him from his ego due to the depression he battled with.

When you are in a state of unhappiness, then this is a negative emotion that creates a block between you and your Spirit team. In a panic, you make reckless decisions that you later regret. As a result, Robert struggled by spending a lifetime of making abrupt choices that ultimately disrupted his path as well as sabotaged others around him who were negatively affected by his choices. When he matured and evolved, he admitted to realizing the negative results that came about due to his past rushed decision making. At that point, he was afraid to make any decisions since they never panned out well. He flew to the opposite extreme by not acting on any of the ideas that came to him out of fear that it won't pan out well. It's an admirable quality to be unafraid to go out there and take a chance on something regardless if you fail or not. In the end, you can say that at least you tried.

Having claircognizance gives one razor sharp thinking abilities. When someone is talking to me about something, I can be listening while also receiving messages filtering through from Heaven. This is the case even if I'm not looking to receive anything. It's usually quick and to the point. When I interrupt and chime in on a conversation, then there are times that what I'm stating is merely relaying what has fallen into my consciousness from above. I don't stop the conversation to dwell incessantly, "Oh, I just got that info from…." Those that know me well already know that some of the things I say are divinely guided, while other times they can tell when it's just me having a personal conversation with them. They are able to distinguish when sudden lightbulb wisdom is being darted at them or if it's just me talking. Some might interrupt, "I know that line was from your Angels."

You may notice the many times throughout your day when you were observing claircognizance in action and how that might have helped you or another in a positive way. Utilizing claircognizance can assist you in knowing if it's the right time to start a new relationship, or a different venture concerning your business or work related endeavors. You'll know if it'll be successful or not. what your next job is intended to be, or if you're on the right path. You know without question what plan God has for you to do and what's intended for the next step of your life. You know this information because it was not only a contract that you agreed to, but the information falls into you naturally through claircognizance. This clair gives you crystal clear upbeat thinking abilities. Pay attention to the thoughts that filter through you each day. Learn to differentiate the ones that come from your ego and the uplifting high vibrational ones coming in from Spirit.

Many writers and authors have a strong degree of claircognizance. They are channeling the words from above. This is regardless if it's a spiritual piece or an entertainment horror thriller book by Stephen King. They naturally fall into a channel zone with spirit as the information and words are dropped into their consciousness. Channeling is a different than being psychic. I can receive random psychic hits without effort sporadically through the day, but to channel for longer periods of time requires a bit of effort and work. Channeling starts with the claircognizance clair as you allow higher beings, entities, spirits to take over your aura and whole being. Lifetimes of knowledge are embedded into your psyche through this process. The channeling energy high is uplifting and overwhelming, but it is energy that ultimately drains you. The process can sometimes take time to raise your spirit into the right higher frequency. To go back home and be on Spirit's vibration is always a joyful enriching experience, but it takes some work to get there and stay in it. When I come back from that space, I more or less collapse wherever I happen to be as energy has been depleted. I need to work on bringing my energy levels back up again. It's a strange euphoric kind of feeling while you're in it, but then it can drop catastrophically when I come out of it. This is because while in the euphoric high vibrational range you are pulled up into Spirit's level, and when you come back out of it you're plopped back into the Earth's physical low vibrational density.

Chapter Five

CLAIRSENTIENCE

Clairsentience means *clear feeling* or *clear sensing*. It is feeling the answers, messages, and guidance coming in from Heaven. Have you ever had a gut feeling or hunch about something specific about to happen, and then it does? Have you felt a sudden strong feeling of joy surrounding an event that you sense is going to happen, and then this ends up coming true? Have you had a feeling of dread or fear overcome you when walking into a room, or that someone is not of a high integrity and that turns out to be true? These are examples of having clairsentience, which is feeling the psychic hits coming through your senses that later proves to be accurate.

Clairsentient beings feel every nuance and vibration within and around them. This can make them doubly sensitive to harsh energies than others, even though everyone is absorbing all of the variations of energies that exist from the good to the bad in their vicinity. The waters of ever flowing feeling within the Clairsentient being are already choppy to begin with because of what it's absorbing every second, so you want to take extra care of your body, mind, and soul. This includes avoiding anything that you sense is not of a higher vibration as well as the people you connect and associate with, to the media you read and absorb. Adopt a strict policy of allowing no drama or negativity in your life as that can send your system through the roof while blocking the true Divine messages flowing through your senses.

Clairsentience is similar to being an empath, but the difference is that an empath has sympathy and compassion for those around them while a clairsentient will *feel* the guidance and messages relayed to them from their Spirit team, but might not necessarily have much concern for another person. Sometimes a Clairsentient being can be so caught up in feeling everything that they can also become hyper focused on those feelings more than the average person. To an extent, it may even be narcissistic without realizing it when the sole focus is on how you feel and what others are doing to you. You may at times drown in it causing you to become moody, irritable, and erratic especially if you have absorbed a whopper of negative vibrations from the physical circumstances around you. This is whether it be in other people or the media.

When circumstances grow extra intense around you, then issues or concerns that were doormat rise up to the surface in a big bad way. It is best to take it easy if possible when that happens. Avoid anything or anyone that easily jars you. This also means steer clear of gossip in all forms of negative media. You are absorbing that energy and becoming one with it even if you're not intending to. It's a narly mess to detangle out of. Use those moments to release anything that doesn't benefit your higher self. Find a spot in quiet nature to detangle and detach from the negative energies you've absorbed. Breathe in the love deeply and exhale out any stresses and concerns giving it to God and your Guide and Angel for positive transmutation.

Falling into gossip or negative media stories or posts is like a temporary drug high. When you're in it, you don't realize that you are. You've grown lost in the thud of those negative energies and no one can pull you out of it except yourself. A similar concept is anyone who has battled an addiction. Many have attempted to help close ones who have fallen into drug or alcohol addiction, but in the end the user has to decide for themselves to want to stop or get help. I've encountered people who don't feel they're committing a crime by complaining about one news story after another on their social media accounts. Whether one likes it or not, complaining energy is negative and helps no one on any level. All of it is toxic to your soul and well-being. It clairvoyantly appears as a dark, black, thick tar around that individual, which blocks that soul from moving forward.

It is one thing to be proactive about something you're against by taking positive steps to produce change, but if you're not doing that, then you're just wasting valuable time that could be used to propel and advance your soul forward. Many receive what seems to be a temporary rush as they fall into negative complaining on social media. They have to keep posting negative rantings to continue to feed their ego while holding their higher self down. It's not helping themselves or anybody else. Those who are highly clairsentient will notice that when they communicate with a constant negative complainer that it just brings them down and makes them miserable. Pay attention to those feelings and notice why they are coming about, then take steps to pull yourself out of that.

An empath is likely to be able to develop their clairsentience channel quite easily if they choose, because half of the feeling and sensing ingredients are already there. If they have concern and sympathy for others, then they have depths of compassionate feelings, which is where the Divine messages flow through.

Earth Angels are a group aligned with having the gift of clairsentience as well. They are generally hyper sensitive and intuitive more than any other. Earth Angels will sacrifice themselves for the well-being of another, but if you are an assertive Earth Angel, then you have learned to no longer accept any form of abuse or hostile environments to be in. You may already have this strict policy in place of not allowing others drama and issues into your environment. This doesn't mean you don't care, but it is taking care of you. You can help a friend going through a problem, but if you find several months have passed and neither of you are moving past the complaint, then it's time to make some healthy life changes.

Incarnated Angels are especially concerned for other people's troubles and will want to help. This can make them prone to falling into the drama and negativity of another. A Star Person may not be sensitive to someone else's issues, but they are still aware the person is struggling and will want to lend a hand. They are good with remaining detached emotionally to the point that others wonder if they have any emotion at all. The Wise Ones are also aware of other people's troubles, but have some measure of detachment to it. They are much stricter about who or how they help. They are the task master Earth Angels and may lecture in the way of helping such as, "Well you knew what you were getting yourself into when you decided to…" And the Incarnated Elementals may be ferociously concerned about someone's troubles to the point of displaying dramatic fiery emotions, but they may not lend a hand unless it is an animal or plant that needs their attention more. Earth Angels in general are incredibly strong even if they or others may not be privy to this strength. They all have a reservoir of clairsentient feeling that rumbles and shakes from within.

The challenge of a clairsentient is coming to terms with how to channel over flowing feelings and senses positively. You absorb every shred of feeling from yourself, from others, as well as the psychic input coming in from above. This includes the good, the bad, and the ugly. It can be so overwhelming that many clairsentients may fall into a pattern of addictions to numb those senses. Whether that be through alcohol, drugs, cigarettes, food, gossiping, or you name it. Anything that is ultimately toxic that they can find to numb it. The ones who don't fall into that pattern may still observe erratic emotions unable to keep them stable. Some may call them, "too sensitive" at times as they might get "touchy" over every little thing that is said.

There are also the tougher warrior like clairsentients who may not get offended over much, but will fall into hard addictions to turn off the over flowing feelings they sense moving through their soul every second. The tougher clairsentients are not afraid to try something dangerously toxic to shut it off. They just need to be aware of when that happens in order to curb it or pull it back to moderation.

Having two to three dominate clairs or more is rare, but I might have gladly handed the clairsentients back. It can be draining constantly feeling and sensing everything and everyone around you every second. It keeps you from partaking in certain activities that seem natural or enjoyable to others. Clairsentient beings will stay away from places that are expected to be crowded. If not, they will go to those places and wonder, "Why did I agree to come here? What was I thinking?" They are the ones who will arrive at a location and notice all of the mobs of people and mumble, "Oh no, why are there so many people?" It's too taxing on their psychic system to be in the midst of that energy. Having clairsentients can keep you from doing practical day to day activities such as a simple grocery store trip or the gym. You start to plan around when you will go to certain places. You likely wouldn't be caught dead going to a mall, promenade, or grocery store at high noon on a weekend day unless you had no choice. Never mind the wear and tear it does to your system sitting in traffic day after day.

It feels like a chore for the clairsentient to go to certain places that seem quite easy for the average person. Clairsentient beings have to learn to be extra careful and cautious in the planning of their daily life. While they might want to go to an amusement park, a movie, or a concert on occasion, they are still super careful about choosing when to do so and with who. The when to go somewhere is not usually on the radar of someone who isn't in tune to the sensitive energies around them. They just go without thinking twice about it that they might appear oblivious to the clairsentient being who would avoid going to say an amusement park when they know it'll be way too crowded. They would also avoid going to see a blockbuster movie on opening night or during its first weekend in a major city.

Being in crowds is too taxing on their equilibrium and the clairsentient prefers to be in nature or away from tons of people. They absorb all of that toxic energy from others like a dirty dish sponge.

All souls should utilize shielding methods to keep toxic energies at bay. This can be by saying something like this at least once a day:

"Archangel Michael, thank you for surrounding with me white light. Allowing only the love to penetrate."

Shield yourself before you head off into areas that you know will have tons of people or negative energies. Shielding is the process of blasting your soul and aura with white light from Heaven. That light is the most powerful light in all existence. I've noticed miraculous shifts and changes when I've shielding compared to not shielding. The shield does wear off after about 12-24 hours so this is something you would need to do daily before heading out to places where there are tampering energies.

Having clairsentients has not typically been a good thing, because I sensed all of the bad and pending dooms too. I could not stand being so sensitive that when I was old enough I began drinking and later turned to drugs and other addictions. I reached for anything that would dull and turn it off for good. My clairsentients was so highly calibrated that it bounced off the Richter scale once the violence in my childhood kicked in. I found there was nothing positive about sensing every feeling that existed. It took me into adulthood to begin seeing that it is a gift that needs to be taken care of.

You know you have clairsentients if you feel and sense every little nuance around you. You are not just feeling and sensing it, but these feelings are giving you a sense of what is going to happen in the future or what has already taken place.

Those who have high clairsentience might walk into a building and feel as if all eyes are on them. Or they will pick up on a sense of foreboding that tells them to get out of a particular place. They perceive danger is about to happen and then it soon does. They also intuit good stuff that is coming into their vicinity as well, which ends up happening. You might have a strong upbeat joyful feeling that the job you want is going to come about, and then this later proves true.

Having clairsentience is when any being in Heaven communicates messages and guidance through your feelings. You get the 'sense' that something is up with someone. You know what they're feeling or going through, therefore you may find that others seem to go to you with their problems. You'll want to be careful of keeping that at bay as much as possible as this can drain your energy and lower your vibration. At the same time, many clairsentient beings tend to get into career fields that including healing or counseling of some kind because of this feeling nature. Ensure you shield before and after these sessions. A clairsentient can also sense if they are in the wrong job. If they work with harsh people or in a hostile environment, then this is a sign to find work that is more aligned with your sensitivities.

A clairsentient might be the kind of person who becomes emotionally upset when someone they're interested in romantically is not reciprocating that interest. You text and email this person regularly hoping to illicit a response that is satisfying to you. Yet, the object of your desire is casual in their reply when communicating with you, or they continuously drop the ball with your text dalliance. You question whether or not they're truly interested in you. When they throw you a bone and click 'like' on one of your social media posts, then you're suddenly on cloud nine believing they're interested in you. Soon you grow upset when a week has passed and you haven't heard from them.

While repeatedly becoming emotionally upset over something like this comes from your ego, the emotional upset you're experiencing is a clairsentient message that this person is not as interested as you were hoping. They might be interested in you on some level, but not in the way you crave. To endure keeping this connection alive will only frustrate and depress you. When they give you a rare 'like' or comment on your social media page, or they text you, then this catapults you into feeling as if this person is deeply interested in you.

Pay attention to your feelings, as this can be the accurate barometer gauge on what is real and what is not. When you move your ego out of the way, you're able to decipher the accuracy of Heaven's incoming messages through clairsentience. You pay attention to others behaviors and are able to intuit what they are telling you. If someone is unresponsive, then this is a sign they have no interest. One might think that this is obvious, but you would be surprised how many people ignore those subtle signs.

Someone with clairsentience can be all over the place when it comes to feelings and emotions. You will want to ensure you work on well-being exercises that keep your emotional balance on an equal footing in order to communicate with Heaven efficiently. With clairvoyance, the clairvoyant will hear someone telling them a story, and will see the story as if it were a movie and actually happening to them. With clairsentience, the person listening to the story will 'feel' what's happening in the story as if it's happening to them. Sometimes if it's a horrific story, the clairsentient may say, "You have to stop." Because the feelings they're experiencing over the story are so overwhelming it's as if it's happening to them.

Gifted actors tend to have highly calibrated clair channels, which enable them to effectively inhabit a character as if they're walking in that person's shoes.

If others accuse you of being too sensitive, then this is a clue that you may have a high degree of clairsentient gifts, which are ready to be awakened. When others find you too sensitive, it can be because every little thing that someone says or does bothers you. Your ego is unable to control your reaction. When you develop your clairsentience and understand how it works, how to shield yourself, then you react less to every shred that comes your way. You incorporate healthy lifestyle changes that keep your emotions on an even keel.

When you have clairsentience, you receive

hunches and gut feelings about situations and circumstances. You might say, "I had this gut feeling that I should've gone the other way instead. I should've listened to it, otherwise this would not have happened."

This is a sign that you're receiving guidance and messages from your Spirit team, but ignored the wisdom being passed through you. Those with clairsentience absorb other people's energy like a sponge. They may find it difficult to be in overcrowded areas. They've complained that it's challenging standing in a store line due to the heavy input of other people's energies. You can sense the emotions and feelings of others and know what feels wrong to you. This can be psychic overload, which is why those with strong clairsentience keep to themselves, avoid negativity, and stay away from crowds or large amounts of people as much as possible.

Because clairsentient beings feel every little nuance around them, this can become uncomfortable and draining even if they're not absorbing negativity. The weight of feelings being absorbed grows too heavy that it has to be wrung out like a sponge packed with water. Take frequent breaks of alone time whenever you can to recharge those batteries. You can sense everything around you from people's emotions to what's to come for someone. Your internal feelings are all over the place like a roller coaster ride. You might give the illusion you are extremely put together on the outside, but on the inside you're wrestling with all sorts of uneasy emotions that constantly ebb and flow like the ocean. You are prone to being a bit jumpy as if someone moved quickly behind you. You turn around to find no one there. Clairsentient people are ridden with anxiety, nervousness, and have a fight or flight response to any and all around them. Imagine absorbing everyone else's feelings being poured into you every second and how that might make you feel.

As a sensitive vibrational being, you will sense things more than the average person would. You enter a store where everyone else seems okay with the energy, yet your Spirit team gives you a warning sign to leave the store. You feel it in your gut area and perhaps your heart rate accelerates. You might hear your Spirit team calmly ask you to leave the store. They ask you to purchase your items somewhere else. Some of these warnings might happen while in a metaphysical store as a reader named Karen explained to me. She believed that because psychics practice there that it must be okay. Unfortunately, that is not always the case. Someone within the store may operate heavily on ego or they are unable to reel the ego in. This can attract in negativity into these stores. Perhaps a hostile client wandered into the store that day and their energy was so intense that it stayed in the store long after they left. You will know if it's not safe if you walk into the store and suddenly you experience negative thoughts or a sudden mood drop.

Other forms of Clairsentience are sensing the presence of a spirit being around you or noticing the air change in certain pockets of a room that cannot be reasoned to be anything else. It can be a hot Summer day, but in one area large enough for a person to be standing or moving about there is a drop in temperature and there is no A/C or fan in that spot. You might feel as if a hand has brushed your neck or arm, and when you quickly whip around you find no one there.

Your gut feelings and hunches are connected to having clairsentience. It can sometimes be tricky deciphering what is real and what is imagined. Imagined or fear based energies are conjured up by the ego and lower self, while Divine communication is uplifting and full of love.

If you're looking for an answer from Heaven on an issue, then ask your question with intention. Afterwards, pay attention to your senses and all that is around you. The answer or message could be coming to you through a voice in your mind out of nowhere, it might show up in a movie, in a song, through a conversation someone is having in passing, or you may feel it through clairsentience.

On March 24, 2015, a *Germanwings* pilot purposely crashed an airplane carrying 150 people killing all aboard. He was not a suicide victim, but a mass murderer who overruled the free will choice and fate of 150 other people. I was jolted awake abruptly from a dream state gasping for air in a panic attack minutes after the plane slammed into the ground. I took a walk outside to get some air and texted one of my best friends to say I was ripped awake with huge dread all over and that I couldn't go back to sleep. I was hearing screams and a heavy machinery impact sound in my

Clairaudience channel, but didn't know what that was. He explained that there was another plane crash before I texted him.

Weeks after the crash all I had been hearing sporadically throughout the day and night was horrific screaming that would not cease. I could not get rid of it as it was jammed tightly in my clairaudience channel. By month two, it gradually and finally began to dissipate.

This isn't uncommon for me, but it messed with my sleep for a good number of weeks reliving what took place leading up to the crash like a recording. This consisted of me being placed into the souls of a different passenger that was on that plane and then taken through what they're experiencing minutes before the crash and leading up to it. This part of the psychic input is coming through clairsentience (clear feeling). This also includes through the eyes and feelings of the children aboard, which is significantly different than the adults. My physical heart races when that passengers heart races. I kept getting ripped awake during sleep in a panic attack hearing the shrieks of horrid screaming, and then I experience the viciously violent impact of the aircraft. It's basically a slaughtering massacre visceral visual from inside the plane, outside the plane, in the cockpit, in the passengers wing, the tearing of the limbs, and on and on. It just plays over and over as if it's repeatedly happening to me. This is from the psychic space I perceive things. When I say that I feel every nuance of everything around me, then you can understand that this is not an understatement.

Not all communication is in a form you would recognize such as a voice (clairaudience), in front of you like a vision (clairvoyance), or in your mind where you just know (claircognizance). Some of it is through your body by feeling the guidance (clairsentience). If you rely on your hunches and intuition when receiving accurate information, then you are feeling the answers, which is clairsentience in action. Trust these gut feelings, as they could be the answered prayer you've been hoping for. Focusing on the stillness within you is where the real truth and answers are.

There are a great many souls who feel every little bit of nuances around them. They can sense the future, but at the same time are feeling and absorbing everyone's energy. Clairsentience beings may fall into self medicating, which can dim or turn off their God given gifts of psychic communication. While some clairsentient's may see the gift as a curse, it is a blessing. It's not God's design to turn off your feeling sense, but at the same time Spirit understands the challenges you face attempting to navigate through a world filled with harsh, cold, toxic, and heartless people. Let's face it, the planet Earth is not creating challenges, but humankind is. If humankind didn't exist, then every inch of Earth would be lush and ripe with majestic natural beauty, perfect breathable air, and a perpetual stream of high vibrational uplifting energy. This stuff exists today on Earth, but is buried beneath the avalanche of toxic negativity created by humankind.

I used to self-medicate with anything and everything possible to turn all of it off. This included drugs, alcohol, and pills. You name it and I likely did it. That didn't go over quite well as you can imagine. There are pluses to knowing what someone is going through just by having them walk past you or stand next to you. You are the one that everyone feels comfortable going to when they want to dump their problems off of themselves. This is why it is absolutely vital you take care of yourself and run your life like a strict executive. Do not be afraid to say, "No, I cannot help or listen to you right now."

Because you feel other's energies and sympathize, you will have to work on being assertive in saying no without guilt. You need to take care of you first, before you can help someone else. You might immediately know whether or not you can possibly help someone or if you should avoid them altogether. You soak up all of that energy including the horrible stuff.

I have to shield every day before I go outside. This is by asking Archangel Michael to surround me with a permeable white light of protection. I also had to train myself to control the flow of emotional information that people outwardly direct at me without realizing it. If you are sensing fear, then mentally call out to Archangel Michael to come in and extract those fears from your body. Those who are clairsentients also have a great deal of empathy and feeling. You are more prone to absorb negativity and/or addictions. When this happens you can invite in entities you cannot see that feed off of you. You may suddenly feel drained or reach for that addiction again. This is why you need to take excellent care of your body and your surroundings more than any other might. Treat yourself delicately and with kid gloves.

I typically avoid places where I know it'll be taxing on my soul energetically. Standing in a crowd of people can make you susceptible to soaking up the tampering energies easily. Oblivious or innocent human souls will stand too close to you and you will absorb that person's energy. Those psychically in tune tend to have trouble with being in crowds because of this. This is because they pick up on all of those frequencies around them. Someone who is oblivious is not very much in tune or aware.

Your soul is so large that it doesn't fit in your body. The light of the soul is six feet all around your human body. Someone is going to be standing in your light. If they are a negative human soul, you will latch onto their toxins while it attaches itself to you. When you arrive back home, you feel drained and crave the need for a nap and do not know why. If a toxic feeling stranger is standing too close to me or a friend is harboring negativity, then I can feel my energy being lowered. This is an example of standing next to someone who is soaked in stress or any other negative emotion. They are called energy feeders because that is what they are essentially doing. They drain you of your high vibrational sensitive energy leaving you worn out or agitated.

You have to be careful that you do not absorb

other people's energy or spend an immense amount of time worrying about them. You will need to train yourself to observe emotional detachment. If you have been in the military or you have had to live at the hands of someone who has abused you, then you likely had developed a good level of emotional detachment. If you are faced with hostile energies, you might react negatively in some way. You might lash out or feel completely drained.

You can work on emotional detachment by breathing in deeply and exhaling until you have calmed down and relaxed. Train your mind to take these incidents that come at you objectively. Also avoid stimulants and heavy amounts of caffeine when possible as that exasperates your nervous system prompting you to be more volatile. When your feelings or thoughts are on overdrive, then this will contribute to stress and depression. This also drains you leaving you feeling tired, even after eight hours of sleep. You constantly reach for caffeinated products to keep going in this fast paced hectic world.

See the innocence and naivety in how someone else might be behaving. Showcasing emotional detachment might make you seem cold or aloof to someone. Pay no mind to any of that and do not feel guilty about it. Reaching for that place of non-guilt is where emotional detachment lives. If you are the go to person where everyone comes to you with their issues regularly, then it is essential for you to practice this emotional detachment.

If you ruminate wondering how to make the

world and the people in it more compassionate, aware, and humane towards one another, then you will need to learn that these are opportunities for you to practice emotional detachment. It doesn't mean you don't care, but everyone is living out their own karma and learning their own lessons. It is not your job to learn those lessons or fix any of that for them. What you can do is BE loving and supportive, but emotionally detached enough that their stuff doesn't get to you and affect your life in a negative way.

Emotional detachment doesn't necessarily mean that you don't allow yourself to feel anything. It means that you separate your emotions from your thinking and take the broader view of a situation to assess it without feeling it. Emotional detachment takes practice, and it's more of a learned skill than an intuitive one.

A clairsentient being feels the answers, messages, and guidance filtering through them from Heaven. The way Heaven communicates with this person is through their feeling sense. Someone who senses something specific that has happened, is happening, or is going to happen is someone who has a strong clairsentient channel. They are super sensitive to every nuance around them.

Everyone has the ability to connect and communicate with a spirit guide or angel. Some see it, others hear it, some feel it, while others know it. Pay attention to your senses as they are communication channels with the other side.

Have it set in your mind that they communicate with you every day. The more you practice, remain aware, and in tune to your senses, then the easier it gets in working with them. You are ceaselessly communicating with them, even if you may not realize the messages you are picking up on are indeed your Spirit team.

Chapter Six

CLAIRALIENCE AND CLAIRGUSTANCE

We covered the four top basic clairs, but there are also many other clairs that exist within one's soul. They are in the minority so we won't cover every single one that is present. However, these next two we'll mention in this brief chapter are Clairalience and Clairgustance.

Clairalience means *Clear Smelling*. Someone with clairalience smells scents that are not happening in real time or on this plane. You might suddenly smell Cedarwood and recall that this was the smell that your Grandmother used to have in her house. Yet, it's coming out of nowhere in the place where you live. This sudden scent around you that is not physically explainable can be that you're picking up on the presence of your Grandmother.

People with Clairalience may smell certain scents out of nowhere that have no rhyme or reason to be smelling this way.

Clairgustance means *Clear Tasting*. This is when you taste anything that is seeping in from the spirit world. You can be lying in bed and suddenly you smell a foreign scent or taste chocolate and yet there is no rational place for the scent or taste to be coming from. You haven't eaten anything resembling chocolate and there are no smells burning anywhere near where you live that could resemble Cedarwood. This is a basic example of how to tell if you have clairalience or clairgustance.

One night I felt extreme thirst, which was odd considering I had just finished drinking a huge tank of water. I eyed my bottle of water, but then something prompted me to crave juice, which rarely ever happens. I buy juice and it sits there. I went into the kitchen and opened the fridge door eyeing the juice selection I had. I heard a hissing noise as I was pulling the juice out and poured it into a cup. I put the juice container back in the fridge and heard the hissing noise again. I opened the fridge and peered in confused looking at the light bulb. "Is that where it's coming from?" I closed the refrigerator door and was startled at the stove on my left. The stove burner was still on! I quickly turned it off, "Oh my god, I'm gassing the place up full of carbon monoxide!"

Had I not received a sudden craving for juice, I would not have gone back into the kitchen until the next morning. It would have been another twelve hours later to find the stove still on or an explosion.

Who knows what would've happened. The thirst *(clairgustance)* and sudden crave for juice was prompted by my Spirit team. I was nudged *(claircognizance)* to head into the kitchen in order to catch this. This may appear so insignificant and slight that someone's ego may discredit it calling it pure luck. When you are fully aware and in tune you start noticing all of the little synchronicities and signs and messages that are put in your path at the right time to help you. You do not notice these signs when you are oblivious or absorbed in your ego. The way your Spirit team guides you is also through these seemingly insignificant situations.

Chapter Seven

CONNECTING WITH SPIRIT

Determining the difference between what is your Spirit team, a high vibrational guide, any being in the spirit worlds that exist, as opposed to your ego and lower self, can be challenging for many Earthly souls. If you're feeling any sort of negative feeling associated with what you believe to be guidance, then it is likely your ego. Yet, a feeling of dread when you walk into a room or place can also signal an accurate warning to leave. On the other hand, there are moments where you could be overly excited about something not realizing that the guidance is your ego, rather than your Spirit team.

You can see how deciphering Heavenly messages can be confusing. One of the main traits is to trust. Trust what you get without worry that you might be wrong. As often as you might think you could be wrong, you could just as equally be right and on the mark. Let go of any struggle and release the worry over whether you are right or wrong. When I've been in a perfect state of calm reception without worry or wonder, then that is when the most accurate messages have taken place. It just flows in naturally without any struggling or wondering.

The obvious way to determine what is Heaven and what is your ego is what ends up panning out in the end. Keep a notebook or journal where you record the hits you get whether ego related or not, then revert back to it on occasion to see what came true. Notice what the circumstances were when you received the hit. You eventually train yourself to understand how the messages come to you.

Don't worry if you get things wrong. That will happen no matter how great your psychic antennae is. Even the most proficient and successful working psychic medium is only about 87% right on a good day. With continued practice, you begin to notice when the guidance you pick up on is more on the mark or not.

When it's *you* talking, then you will hear the word, "I". It will be bathed in dark ego or negativity such as, "I'm not qualified for that job."

When it's your Guide or Angel, then you will hear the word, "You". It will be direct and immersed in love and optimism. This voice will say something like, "*You* will obtain that job as *you* are more qualified than you realize."

The guidance, information, and messages from spirit have high vibration energy to it. It is also filled with uplifting love that assists you or someone else in a positive way. If you are riled up in anger, then that is your ego, since heavenly communication is bathed in calm love even if it's a warning. The chatter in your mind causes confusion and chaos pushing you to act on the voice of ego. If you feel you're receiving messages urging you to create negative disruption in your life, or to hurt yourself, or harm someone else in any fashion, then that is the chatter in your mind and not God. Voices from spirit are direct, optimistic, and filled with compassion and love, even if it's sending you a warning.

You may find that there are certain circumstances that rile you up in anger. For example, if you're someone who grows extremely angry whenever you discover trash littered all over creation. This is a hint as to what your life purpose and soul passion is. Taking positive action that can help stop littering is what your goal is. You channel that anger into something positive that can change things. Complaining or protesting about it won't do much in the way of preventing it from happening, so you look for other ways you can help create positive change in that arena.

The feeling of being trapped at times is another sign of one having high psychic abilities. You're more in tune than those who operate primarily from their ego. The trapped feeling is also you absorbing the harsh energies being darted around this planet. You're absorbing it without intending to and this causes a suffocating feeling.

Your psychic antennae will fluctuate up and down throughout the day depending on your mood and state of mind. Pay attention to when those moments happen during your day, then adjust your well-being state accordingly to get you re-centered again. Watching what you consume into your body will help, as well as getting out into a calm serene nature setting to help remove stresses and toxins that have attached themselves to your aura.

Incorporate daily exercises that work for you in order to strengthen your connection with Spirit. When in doubt pray for help and guidance on how to become more in tune. Develop a relationship with your Spirit team, even if you don't believe in it right away. Soon enough you'll start to notice signs of their presence. Your guides and angels assist you in a myriad of ways. It isn't just to help you get that great job or awesome love. They help with day to day stuff too! There is nothing too small or trivial for them to step into help you with. This can be little things like locating an object you lost somewhere in your house, to clearing the path when you jog the streets, to surrounding your car with white light to ensure you're safe while driving. They help re-center you and bring your soul to the space of peace. They can also help in detaching you from drama and keeping you focused on your path. They help you in understanding someone's true nature and why circumstances take place.

You are born with profound gifts of psychic insight, which you must come to terms with and understand. You have all of the answers within, so this is a matter of trusting those answers. Recognize these visions to be true and continue to practice and learn how to accurately decode them.

It's like riding a bike or any other chore. The more you do it, the better you become!

Chapter Eight

PRAYER AND AFFIRMATIONS

So many struggling to make ends meet, struggling to get by, struggling uphill period. This isn't unusual as humankind has infinitely struggled throughout Earth's history to achieve peace and happiness. That's one thing that most everyone can agree on. The goal is the same and that is to be happy. Even the permanent miserable grumps deep down at their soul essence long for that joyful content feeling. It makes you feel good and blasts away any moody irritable unhappiness.

As you read this now, I surround you with the Light of the Holy Spirit as well as angels who are of 100% pure uplifting love and to help in raising your vibration and to assist you along your life's path and purpose.

When in doubt, ask for help from above, even

if you don't see evidence of movement. If your faith wavers due to lack of evidence, then ask to have your faith boosted. Miracles happen daily as Guides and Angels in Heaven work tirelessly guiding every soul on the planet to make life a little more pleasant. That's seven billion souls living an Earthly life with at least one guide and one angel per person. That's at least 14 billion spirit beings guiding every human soul on the planet. They can only do so much. Their job is to guide you, not hand you everything the second you ask for it. They are also dealing with the free will choice of human beings. Most people are not that in tune to the guidance and messages coming through from above, nor do they understand how to recognize it, yet each and every soul has the strong capacity for receiving incredible psychic hits.

It's not like Heaven can drop a bucket of cash on everybody's doorstep as much as many people would rather enjoy that. What would everyone learn if that were the case? Those who are well to do financially are also not exempt from troubles I can assure you. If something isn't forthcoming, then there are reasons beyond what you cannot comprehend or understand at the time. There are also circumstances and experiences that you need to be enlightened about on your own.

Sometimes heavenly assistance is not forthcoming for a variety of reasons. It could be that you are being guided to take action steps that will help move you out of the stagnancy you're in, but you're either not picking up on this guidance, or you have fear surrounding this move since it might feel like it's moving you out of your comfort zone. You fear a negative repercussion, but of course, no high vibrational spirit being in Heaven will guide you into a disaster. What might seem like a scary move could be the one that ends up moving you upwards.

I have forever believed in the power of prayer. This is not because it's taught in some circles to do. This is because I have witnessed miraculous intervention and changes in my own life as well as for others only after I prayed. When I did nothing, then nothing changed. When I asked for assistance or prayed, then I noticed positive changes come about. I wouldn't continue with anything unless I knew it worked. This is why I have been a lifelong advocate of prayer.

Sometimes Divine intervention happens immediately, while other times the assistance isn't forthcoming right away, but with those cases I have noticed it eventually comes to fruition at some point. I have incorporated daily prayer throughout the course of my entire life because it works.

Many are usually surprised over the humor that pops in and out at times while talking to Heaven. That's because Heaven is not some stern, harsh, cold place. It's filled with uplifting love, peace, and joy. Those are qualities that all beings in Heaven exude. They are bathed in those energies, which equates to also having immense humor. You can then likely gather that this is how they view circumstances in the practical based Earthly world. They see most of what goes on in a humor filled light rather than the tragic offended manner that many on Earth view circumstances around them in.

Some atheists or non-believes do not believe in prayer, but they're also unaware that they are praying without realizing it. I've heard of cases where a non-believer takes time out each day to sit with their thoughts. In that instance, they are communicating with God whether they believe they are or not. You are a piece of God. Every atom and cell that exists in all dimensions is Him.

You can use prayer to boost your faith, reduce fear, and give you crystal clear psychic perception. Prayers are much like affirmations in that it is the intention behind the words that have weight. The stronger your intention within your prayers, then the brighter the light around it is.

Heaven sees affirmations and prayer as lights being shot upward into the Universe. These lights are of varying shades. Some prayers have a brighter and stronger light around them, while other prayers appear dimly lit if it's a prayer or affirmation that has ego based property energy within it that benefits no one except the ego. Other times the dimly lit prayers can be requests that are not considered urgent. It could be you really want that brand new tech gadget that the store just received, whereas a brighter lit prayer would be coming from someone who is in immediate physical danger.

Children's prayers tend to have some of the brightest lights around them. Part of that has to do with the fact that most Children have not become jaded and are believing in a higher power, whereas an adult might have some doubt energy within their prayer, which actually darkens the light being shot into the air. Asking for a boost in faith strengthens this light within the prayer.

My mother taught me how to pray from back in the day when I was a child. Before bed she would eventually make her way into our room to lead us in prayer. There was no judgment or negativity associated with these prayers at all. She is an incarnated angel, so those prayers were bathed in 100% compassion for all people. My mother's faith eventually waned over the years and my father struggled to have some resemblance of faith. It was ironic that in an extended family that I had the most faith that would only grow stronger as I moved into adulthood. Part of this was due to the fact that I could hear my Spirit team, so I knew there was something bigger than the physical plane that existed. I mainly grew up in a home of atheists and agnostics, but as I grew more vocal with my teachings many of the family members slowly awakened their skepticism. The point of that is I wasn't influenced by anyone around me growing up when it came to my spiritual beliefs. It was Heaven that heavily influenced me.

Many people sometimes feel as if they're not loved by the Divine, or that they're being ignored, neither of which are true. All are loved and no one is ignored. When it feels that way, then that has to do with your feelings, which ebb and flow. Feelings are not incessantly accurate when it's a reaction generated by the ego. The best way to feel loved by the Divine varies from one person to the next, but you can start by increasing your faith, having regular prayer, and conversations with the

Divine, even if it feels like you're talking to no one. You are heard and eventually you start noticing the signs that you're not alone and that you are loved. In the physical world, the ego requires physical concrete material evidence of that love, but the love is felt from within like a great big warm hug.

I find all forms of prayer have worked and have been equally successful for me. This is regardless if it's hands clasped together, in meditation, in writing, or while in motion. There hasn't been one method that works better than the others. This is because it doesn't matter how you do it, but that you do it. The most immediate way of receiving answers in a prayer is while in a calm state of mind, which means that sometimes the response will come about long after the prayer was executed.

Have the intention that you will clearly hear, see, feel, and know the messages and guidance Heaven wishes to relay to you. Visualize crystal clear bright white light shining onto the clair you wish to awaken from slumber. Imagine the white light blasting away any and all of the toxic dark debris that may have accumulated on it.

The clair senses within all souls are nothing unusual, because it is through those senses that the spirit and soul communicate with one another back home on the other side. Soul mates or couples that are super tight on Earth have a telepathic communication between one another where they are able to sense what the other is going through or thinking. Some people have joked that they wished they could read someone's mind. Well, back home in Heaven, that is how others communicate with each other. There are no lies created, because everyone already knows the truth.

You may also call upon a specific Archangel to assist in opening up your various clair channels:

Archangel Uriel - Claircognizance (clear knowing)
Archangel Haniel - Clairsentience (clear feeling)
Archangel Zadkiel - Clairaudience (clear hearing)
Archangel Raziel - Clairvoyance (clear seeing)

Chapter Nine

PSYCHIC PREDICTIONS COME TRUE

The way I read others is by combining all of my clair channels as illustrated in the upcoming examples.

I was on the phone reading for an inquiry. I breathed in and out mentally asking my team for any messages on him. Purple forms and shapes came at me. Seeing violet colors is common when your Third Eye Chakra *(clairvoyance)* is open or in the process of opening.

I said, "I am shown a red car and a guy with brown hair driving it."

He asked, "What kind of car?"

Hearing the word through my clairaudience channel I said, "Ford."

I continued on describing the clairvoyant pictures I was seeing. "The weather shows the sun is out, but it's cold. People are bundled up and rushing around in heavy coats. There are tall buildings around, so it looks like a big city. There is a subway or trolley rushing by above ground."

He said, "I think you're talking about my brother. He has brown hair. He just bought a red Ford Focus and he's in Chicago right now. They have a train that is above ground."

Hearing through clairaudience I asked, "Who is Michael?"

He said, "That's him. That's my brother. He's the one you saw with the car."

Then through my claircognizance and sense of knowing channel I said, "Okay, he's moving or wants to move from where he lives."

He said, "Yeah, he's in Chicago, but has mentioned moving to San Diego. I don't know how serious he is about that."

There are times when just enough information is revealed, but you are not shown the entire picture. One of the reasons is sometimes you're only picking up on pieces of the psychic input. Some of the information gets lost as its transmitted from one spiritual plane to another. You're not getting the whole drawn out circumstance or message. The other reason is that your Guides and Angels will not live your life for you. They may offer suggestions, but then it is up to you to figure out what is the best course of action. If you make a mistake, then they will help you out when you ask them to intervene. Your life will brighten in beautiful ways when you invite your Spirit team into your house.

Those not understanding how psychic

phenomena works automatically assume that if someone is psychic then they should be able to know every single detail about someone. That is just not accurate when in the Earthly plane. You pick up pieces here and there through the dense distractions of the physical world, but you rarely get every tiny shred. A super great psychic medium is versed and practiced enough to string the pieces together when reading.

It is not necessarily fun when you know *(claircognizance)* the person you're in a relationship with is straying. When I was twenty-nine years old, I was in a relationship with someone who was not faithful. My guides showed me the soul mate I was with at the time in a moving vision *(clairvoyance)* along with a dark figure in the background. They told me there was someone else in the picture with us that I was not seeing. Weeks later I discovered it was true and I left the relationship.

A friend calls and says with blunt tactlessness, "I'm in love with someone...." As he spoke, his voice trailed off into the background when I took a huge deep breath in, exhaled, and mentally said, "Show me the person he's talking about." The image popped up in front of me and I opened my eyes interjecting, "It's a guy. Dark hair. Fit. There's a tattoo on his arm and he's got one on his back." My friend was silent for a beat absorbing it then said, "Yeah. His hair is black. And he does have a tattoo, but it's wrapped around his arm and extends along the side and onto his back. It's one piece."

What can you pin point out that I did to make this happen? All I did was take a huge deep breath releasing any stresses. Why? It helped relax me and move me into a slightly altered state. When I'm in a relaxed state, then it's easier for me to connect. It's the relaxed state that helps form the connection. I didn't struggle for hours. Everything I mentioned took less than 60 seconds. The deep breath inhale, and then exhale release, then formed the question to my Spirit team, they then answered me by revealing an image through Clairvoyance. They could've simply spoken it through Clairaudience and I would've heard it clearer, but they chose to show the visual instead. I reported back what I saw and it was confirmed. My friend later sent me photos of this person that matched what I saw. He wasn't all that surprised considering he's known me for years and is used to me chiming in with messages.

I've never understood the strange exercises that are taught to connect at times. It's the same way I've never understood taking an acting class to pretend to be a tree. This scenario described is one of billions of hits that sift in and out all day long throughout each day and night of my life randomly without any effort.

You have access to Divine information about others when you are in tune to the vibrations within and around you. Breathe, relax, and connect with the other side. You'll be amazed at the messages you receive when you practice connecting regularly.

There are times where you might not know if it is your imagination or your Spirit team. When I was a child I would sometimes wonder who was talking to me. I grew to understand that I'm super hard on myself, so that's how I am able to tell the difference between what's me and what is a higher being communicating with me. Your Guides and Angels do not give you a hard time. You give yourself the hard time. This is your ego and how you differentiate. Your ego wants to make you uncomfortable and insists that you are incapable of doing anything.

Knowing that you are not alone and that there are Spiritual beings on the other side assisting you to have a peaceful life full of abundance takes practice, faith, and trust. I have off days as we all do, but I'm fully aware of those days. I pray to release the burdens that I accumulate as it comes. I have battled trying to connect with so much going on in my mind that it's impossible to shut it off. There was a time in my earlier life where I had ego interference over whether or not I was on the right path just like anybody else. I would be working on writing pieces where I'm blocked and experiencing a blank slate, then when I'm knee deep in it I would wonder if I was making a mistake. You can see how the lower self wants to argue with your true higher self and delay you from doing anything.

Using divination tools are exceptional ways to confirm what you're getting. There are endless choices for divination tools that people use in order to communicate with spirit from Tarot and Oracle decks, to runes, stones, crystals, pendulums, and so on. For Tarot or Oracle card decks, search online for images of the different cards available to see what resonates strongly with you. This is especially valuable if Clairvoyance isn't your stronger clair as your team can show you an image from a card in order to convey what they're attempting to relay to you. One of the most basic Tarot decks others start off with is the traditional Rider-Waite Tarot deck. The Tarot can be complex to learn, but I break down the general meanings to help you narrow it down in my book, *Tarot Card Meanings*.

One client informed me that she wanted to look at love relationships. She said she was dating two guys simultaneously and wanted to know which one is the guy. Without using a card deck, I repeated what I heard my Spirit team said through Clairaudience, "Neither."

I added *(clairvoyance)*, "It looks like one of the guys is older than you and the other one is younger."

She confirmed this to be true that she is in her thirties and one of the guys was in his twenties, while the other was in his forties.

I informed her that there was another guy that was going to enter the picture, but that I didn't see him becoming anything until about a year from the point of the reading. This information came to me through clairvoyance when I saw the visual of the following year being circled on the calendar. I picked up on the energy of another guy through clairsentience.

The next move I made was by double checking this information or any other messages that needed to come through with a Tarot deck. While I shuffled, my Spirit team audibly requested that I pull two cards. I threw down the Empress and the Hierophant.

I said, "Yes, he is the guy. I received a double yes."

I went further and added, "There will be marriage (Hierophant) and a pregnancy (Empress) with this guy."

A year later, I had forgot all about the reading, but the woman came back to tell me I had read for her. She said didn't believe the read at the time, but changed her tune when she found everything I stated was taking place exactly a year from the reading. She informed me that the two guys she was originally dating were both no longer in the picture, and that a new guy popped up with who she had a deeper connection with. She added that they have plans to get married and have a child.

PRESIDENTIAL PREDICTIONS

I have accurately predicted every single United States President elect in my current lifetime to date. This includes Bill Clinton, George Bush, Barack Obama, and Donald Trump. I've nailed it early on more than a year and a half out before the results came to light. One of the reasons is that I'm emotionally detached from the outcome of a Presidential Election, whereas a great number of people are not. They are deeply and passionately mired into its toxic energy, which creates a block. When I say I'm emotionally detached, it means that I don't care. I have zero emotion involved with it.

You cannot favor one candidate with great

fervor over another and receive accurate psychic results. It's near impossible because of the blocks erected by being emotionally invested into what you're psychically reading about. It's the same way some readers are unable to read for themselves as they are too close to the situation to see clearly. It is also why there are psychic readers who won't read for friends or people they know because they have some measure of an emotional attachment to them. It becomes a conflict of interest in a sense.

Everyone connects to the Other Side in various ways. As a clairaudient, it can sometimes be like tuning into a station on the radio. I can hear the static in one ear as I'm tuning in and moving the dial until I hear my Spirit team clearly. This is how I heard about the 2008 Election from Heaven. My Spirit team stated that Hillary Clinton would not make it to the finish line. It will be Barack Obama and John McCain as the nominees, but Barack Obama will be the President elect.

I also heard the same information for the 2012 United States Election trajectory and outcome over a year prior. With all of the noise in the world arguing about it, I tuned that out and heard the real voices of Heaven break it down for me.

In November 2011, through clairaudience, my Spirit team listed each of the running candidates that were dropping out of the race in order, which later came to pass in that order. I said that Mitt Romney and Barack Obama would be the Presidential nominees, which no one believed at the time. There was talk and arguments among the media and social media hyper-focusing on Michele

Bachmann and Rick Santorum as being the Republican nominees. If they were tuned into Spirit, they would have been able to see that it just wasn't going to be true.

Michele Bachmann dropped out in January 2012 followed by Rick Santorum in April 2012 as my forecast predicted. My Spirit team told me that Mitt Romney would not make it. Barack Obama will be the United States President in 2012 for a second term, which later proved to be accurate.

My mind then drifted off wondering what an incredible place this would be if politicians and its people were all in tune to their own Guides and Angels. Not only would there be peace on Earth, but no one would waste years obsessing over a political election because they would already know who is soul contracted to be the next President at that time in Earth's history. They would instead focus on more important positive life purpose endeavors instead of the drama and noise of the physical world that leaves you spinning in a merry go round indefinitely.

My most controversial psychic prediction stated was when my Spirit team informed me about the November 2016 election results in my column blog dated back in August of 2015.

What I posted up was that the two Presidential nominees were going to be Hillary Clinton and Donald Trump. This was predicted at a time when most everyone saw neither reaching the finish line and no one seemed to want them. I relayed the messages my Spirit team gave me while in a calm emotionally detached state. I stood by that without bending.

At that time, people were heavily fixated on Bernie Sanders, Ted Cruz, and Marco Rubio as the front runners. If psychic engines were running at optimum levels for those disappointed and shocked by the ultimate results, then they would've known what was going to be taking place. They would have worked on accepting it and realizing that things take place the way they do for a reason. Actually, they wouldn't have been that emotionally obsessed about it to begin with. Emotional obsession creates a block between soul and Spirit beings in Heaven, because the emotions fall into negativity, and as stated negative anything is a block.

After my Spirit team gave me the nominees, they informed me through clairaudience and then a clairvoyant vision of what was to come. It was a visual of Donald Trump with one hand raised and one hand over the Bible. I took that to mean one thing: Donald Trump would be voted in as the United States President in November 2016. I double and triple checked with my go to Tarot deck and received the Knight of Wands. The Knight of Wands shows a vivacious restless fiery individual who accomplishes whatever it sets out to do. They can also be bold and tactless at times without concern for others feelings, but they will get the job done that they set out to do. I triple checked again with Hillary Clinton and Bernie Sanders, and I received endless negatives. They would not be the next President.

This big psychic prediction came true stunning

those who passionately opposed Donald Trump, and were sure he would never become President. It was their ego that was sure, because ones higher self knows the psychic truth. If they had paid attention to what I posted up eighteen months prior to the election, then they would've seen the trajectory laid out over how it would play out. We can go one step further by saying never mind reading it from me, if they had tuned into their Spirit team from way back when, then they would have received the information themselves.

If this was you, then look at the emotions you were expressing during the election cycle. Notice the negative energy associated with that and how that prevented you from seeing the results clearly. It can be challenging trying to break down what is negative energy and what isn't, because many would likely insist they weren't being negative, but passionately did not want him as President. By saying you don't want something, then you're moving into negative energy and you're saying, "Bring me this thing I do not want."

Being centered and balanced without judgment is by saying, "This is a democracy and I will accept whatever comes about even if it's not my personal favorite choice. Events take place for a reason that are beyond my understanding or control. I will not allow the results of a presidential election to permanently scar and upset me."

In December 2016, my message box was blowing up from people telling me that another one of my psychic predictions a month prior was accurate again. This prediction was having to do with the United States Electoral College and recount controversy with the hopes and intentions of some of his detractors desiring to stop the 2016 United States President Elect Donald Trump from taking office after he was elected. As I tuned into Spirit, and within a matter of seconds, I already knew that wouldn't happen and that it's a done deal, which is what I informed those posing me the question, "Will stopping the electoral college work?"

No human being has the power to stop something that was pre-contracted to take place to begin with. This means the answer is no and it ended up being no in the end as predicted. I continued to stand by the psychic prediction during the long drawn out election process. Instead I ignored the drama and focused heavily on my work and other activities. I would double check the prediction here and there for those passionately wanting to know, but the answer from my Spirit team was always the same. What you can do is work on accepting an outcome you're displeased with and focus on positive ventures to assist in moving humanity forward. In fact, don't allow yourself to get weighed down by the negativity of gossip, media, and political candidates to begin with. Everything always ends up well in the end and no one is in any true danger. Fear is a deceptive blindfold preventing you from diving deeper into the truth.

Donald Trump became the United States President in November 2016 as I psychically predicted. The original prediction was so farfetched and believe me I was out there alone with that one because many professional working psychics who read for a living did not foresee it. They were calling Bernie Sanders or Hillary Clinton. The reason they were unable to accurately predict something like that was because they were too emotionally invested in the gossip and negativity surrounding the election. They fell prey to the allure of human events and it is the job of a psychic reader to not become invested emotionally in judgment over something they're psychically reading about. It skews your psychic perception as was proven when Donald Trump was sworn into office.

This is to illustrate out how and what can create a block with the Divine. Masses of people were emotionally invested and negatively affected in a world event circumstance that they were unable to clairvoyantly see what was predestined to take place at that time in history. This was one of the largest global events that created so much never-ending negativity out of people that I and all in Heaven has ever witnessed. It was a tragic moment in history to see so many allow themselves to become that permanently negatively associated to an event, when it would have been more understandable if emotional upset had risen over a tragic human situation that needs attention such as poverty, depression, violence, killings, lack of love, and child abuse.

When one is absolved in negative emotions, then you do not know, feel, see, or think clearly while in that state. You cannot favor one situation over another and be in tune to the psychic truth. You cannot be mired down in any shred of negative emotion and be in tune. You cannot be obsessed with reality T.V. or gossip surrounding celebrities and be in tune. It's near impossible as it becomes a conflict of interest and blocks you from picking up on the valid psychic information coming through from above.

When I inject personal emotions into a situation, then I can be inaccurate. This would be interpersonal relationships, which I have more understandable deeper emotions involved in. When you're in tune to the vibrations coming in from beyond, then you can clearly receive the psychic truth. You'll note through this illustration how strong and influential negative fear and worry energy can be. Fear comes from the darkness of ego, which poorly clouds your psychic judgment.

In order to accurately predict psychic information, you need to be completely emotionally detached from the situation. Remain quiet, calm, peaceful, serene, and emotionally removed from the nonsense. Stay centered in the drama and be the calm in the eye of the hurricane around you in order to tune in accurately to worlds beyond. Offer more constructive and helpful tips on how to rise above negativity and find the center of certainty where love resides. Understand that even a liar has their own truth and without judgment come to this truth. Avoid falling into the deceptive ego's trick of coming from a place of fear, which clouds judgment and only attracts more of that energy to you.

Chapter Ten

I AM PSYCHIC AND SO ARE YOU!

$\mathcal{I}$ am psychic and so are you! All souls are created equally and no one is more special than any other. A soul might incarnate into a human body on the Earth plane and appear visually different from another soul within its physical casing, but the soul itself is made up of the same substance as all souls. It incarnates into a human body to live an Earthly life with others who appear and act differently than they do. Part of the reason for this is in order to teach that soul to love and accept someone for their differences. If everyone appeared and acted exactly the same, how boring would that be?! Yet, that is what the ego desires. It wants everyone to look, act, and support the same as it does or else there will be Hell to pay.

The planet would be a beautiful uplifting joyful place to be if every soul was operating from their true highest vibrational nature full time and around the clock. Unfortunately, that is not realistic due to the fact that the darkness of ego in humankind has made the planet a negative place to be living on. It turned Earth into a ticking time bomb on the fringes of exploding. It is a place ruled by greed, power, hatred, violence, and pain. Humankind is to blame for ensuring the planet remains in that negative state.

Obsessing over media stories will block your psychic radar. This applies to those who fall into the negative gossip about celebrity, entertainment, and politics. If you spend your days attacking political candidates or celebrities, then you have erected a thick block between your Spirit team and your communication with them. When you consistently complain about a political candidate you don't like, or a celebrity you despise, or someone you don't support, then you have contributed to the negative energy state of the planet. Note the word, "consistently", meaning you do it once or twice, then it won't create that much of a dent, but multiply that with doing it regularly and with everyone else who is doing the same thing, and how often you're doing it, then you've got a disaster of toxic energy flooding the etheric atmosphere around Earth.

Are you a regular offender? Or did you allow it to slip out in conversation casually without malice a few times? The emotion behind the words adds weight to how large of a contribution it is. The more negative feeling the emotion is, then the more polluted the energy is being darted into the atmosphere. If you're communicating positive uplifting words about these things, then you are doing your part in uplifting the vibrational energy around the planet into that of love.

What did the cartoon character in the Disney film *Bambi* say? If you can't say anything nice, then don't say anything at all. It's as basic as that positive mantra that has more or less been worded and re-worded over the centuries by those who desire others to be bathed in love and joy around the clock. They understand that being around a *Negative Nancy* just brings you down. Who wants to be around that? The ego does for one. The angels have joked that they are happy to mace anyone with white Light who is permanently stuck in the dark toxic cesspool of negativity, which is not a pleasant place to live.

Feeling any kind of negative emotion for a prolonged period of time will block Heavenly communication. This means if you're living under constant stress, heavily depressed, or perpetually angry. Those are the kinds of emotions that dim and block the communication line with the other side. This is also why working psychics and mediums typically take fifteen minutes or less before starting their readings for the day to relax, re-center, and turn the noise around them off. This way they can efficiently connect with the other side for accurate messages for that client.

You are a soul in a temporary human body with emotions, feelings, and thoughts you are wrestling with every second. Believe me I can relate, having incarnated into a human family this lifetime with depression, anxiety, and suicidal tendencies right down my Mother's genetic line. I've battled depression and negative thoughts on occasion just like any other. I'm not immune to falling down that rabbit hole, but I'm consciously aware of it and doing my best work to climb back out as quickly as possible because I know in the end it doesn't help me. I also know that it's not necessarily something that someone can control. It can take a lifetime battling mental disorders. I've had lifelong anxiety and social anxiety over depression. The social anxiety was brought upon by an abusive childhood upbringing at the hands of a violent parent. The extreme social anxiety and anxiety symptoms were not present when I was born. They were engrained during my human development days. I understand what it's like to battle with mental disorders, but this isn't the same as falling into a perpetual pessimistic path about what's in the media. If I were a pessimist, I could never have accomplished the things I set out to do over the course of my life, even after I was told by numerous parties I couldn't do it. I paid no mind and went after what I was intended to do and accomplished it. You can too!

A high vibrating soul can do their best to ensure they steer clear of drama by working hard to set up their life in a way that has minimal contact with the nonsense of physical life. The further you are away from the noise, then the stronger your psychic frequencies are.

The soul is a highly calibrated psychic machine that fluctuates up and down while inside the human body on the Earth plane. When it's in the spirit world, it stays highly calibrated, but when on the Earth plane it bounces around all over the place due to the dense heavy thick atmosphere that surrounds the planet. Most of the particles that exist in this density is created by every soul on the planet by negative actions and thoughts. If the atmosphere is this extremely dense, then you can imagine how awful and toxic so many souls are in the way they act and think on a daily basis. It shouldn't be a surprise to anyone as to how bad it is, because all you have to do is log online to the Internet and skim gossip media sites and comments. Visit social media sites like Twitter, Instagram, or Facebook and you'll get a pretty good idea over how bad it is. The culprits and offenders are blind to the temporary rushed high they're wallowing in and are unaware they're doing anything wrong. It's the same way an abuser denies having abused anyone when an accusation is made. Holding a mirror up to oneself with objectiveness can help in seeing how bad one might be acting out. I've heard people tell others who act out, "You should watch yourself on video to see how bad you are with others. It might wake you up."

Luckily, there are many immensely awesome high vibrational light workers who know their purpose and reason for incarnating during any particular time in history. They have chosen to steer clear of the drama and noise of the physical life and limit their posts and dealings to ones that are uplifting, empowering, and inspirational. They do their best to remain centered as much as possible in the eye of the hurricane.

Every soul has clairs (clear senses) and chakras (energy points) that move up and down, and expand in and out. It acts like a gauge depending on where that soul's consciousness is at and what kind of emotions that soul is experiencing at any given moment during its existence. If you are riding sky high on love and joy, then your vibration raises. When your vibration raises, then so does your psychic antennae. If you are in the throes of any negative emotion, including complaining or whining about someone else, or what's being done to you, or how something upsets you, then this drops your vibration, and lowers your psychic frequency. It's just the way the soul is designed vibrating with varying colors and shades of the rainbow. It can glow a vibrant green color as it experiences healing, to an uplifting joyful bright yellow, to a purifying white, and then to the darkest shade of toxic black. This is all in the span of an hour depending on what that soul is experiencing in its life. If their emotions and moods fluctuate, then so does the psychic antennae.

It is the soul's goal to be aware of that and conscious of it. Knowing what will wear them down and what will enhance it. When you discover you've slipped into a low vibration, then work on raising your vibration again. Even the most compassionate loving person will slip into a low vibration. Sometimes it's not even at your own hands. You could be in line at a grocery store absorbing negative energies without realizing it, or you hear someone arguing with venom, or a friend darts gossip at you, or you read a negative post on social media, then your vibration begins to drop and you didn't intend for that to happen. You were minding your own business high on life and then the negative energies infiltrated you. When that happens, then work on re-raising your vibration, clearing your space, centering, and grounding yourself.

Over the centuries, it has been taught to believe that having psychic gifts are only for a select chosen few. The reality is that every soul is born with these gifts and capabilities of being a conduit with the other side, including the ones that are completely closed off and blocked to it. The more psychic hits you receive throughout the day will give you a clue as to when you are operating with a high vibration and when you're on a lower vibrational playing field. It is raising your vibration that gives one clearer psychic reception.

A Medium is someone who acts as a vessel of communication with the other side. Spirits on the other side live in a world that is high vibrational, which also means they have a high vibration. It's much easier to have a high vibration in the spirit world than it is in the practical world since the soul's natural state of being is high vibrational to begin with. The spirit world is bathed in high vibrational energy. There are no wars, hatred, anger, hating, or harming of any kind back home. It is 100% pure love, joy, and peace.

The spirit in Heaven has a high vibrational state of being and a human soul has a lower vibrational state even when operating at its highest potential. This can make the psychic connection challenging on Earth. This is also why even the best psychics will only receive pieces of information coming through that later prove to be accurate. They're not receiving the whole picture at times because their vibration is attempting to connect with the higher vibrational energy in the spirit world.

When the Medium wishes to make a stronger connection, they will work on raising their vibration to a higher state, and their Spirit team will begin to lower their vibration in order to reach the Medium. They are meeting the Medium conduit halfway, hence the word *Medium*, which is the half way mark.

A Medium is psychic, but a psychic is not a Medium. Every soul is born psychic and has varying degrees of this ability, but that does not equate to being a Medium. A Medium communicates with spirits or those who have crossed over. They are able to gain broader access from the other side than a psychic can. While a psychic may receive random communication hits about the future, what's taken place, or is taking place. This is the basic difference between a psychic and Medium. Once you've awakened your psychic gifts, then it is easier to take that next step and make a spirit connection as a Medium.

Spirit helps by giving you what your soul needs in order to continue on its path. This means they don't necessarily give you what you want. There are reasons you are enduring challenges. While some of the challenges are at your ego's hand and by your own doing, other challenges are placed on your path for a reason that might include enlightening you in a way that helps you grow and evolve.

This is part of the reason a psychic can't give someone the winning lottery numbers. Naturally that would make someone's day especially those who are struggling financially. If Spirit gave 7 billion people on the planet the winning lottery numbers, then imagine what kind of disasters would come out of that. Spirit gives you what you need, and not always what you want. The lottery numbers are computer generated and chosen through free will. Spirit is unable to override the free will choice of a human being unless it is to prevent their death before the time that was soul contracted.

In Heaven, all souls are of service balancing both work and play. This is what they desire of human souls who seem to do more work than play, or the opposite end of the spectrum more play and no work. They are against human souls who primarily work without play, and the flipside extreme of all play and no work. This also means even if they could, they wouldn't be passing out the winning lottery numbers to people anyway, especially to those souls who are not ready for it. Having boundless money flowing in does not equate to happiness as there are a great many people who are financially well off and are still not happy or are struggling in other areas.

While in reality having enormous financial flow does help with the practical necessities required in life this is true, but it doesn't equate to being happy. You could achieve that and may possibly be happier than the drudgery of having to work at a job you despise, yet if your soul isn't operating on a higher vibrational playing field, then misery sets in.

Spirit understands that human souls on Earth need money in order to survive on the planet. You primarily need clothes, food, and housing, but you desire love. Spirit will help each soul on the planet to ensure they are taken care of to the best that they can pending you invite them in to work with you since they cannot interfere in another soul's life unless specifically requested by that soul. They will guide you in action steps to take that will lead you closer to obtaining enough income to ensure you are living comfortably and at peace. This means guiding you to meaningful work that is aligned with your equilibrium. One that will make you happy to do. The cold structured 9-6 Monday thru Friday corporate world is not for everyone, and certainly not conducive to a sensitive soul. As it stands, Heavens view has been that the cold structured corporate worlds are in drastic need of re-structuring for morale alone. If you dread going into work each day, then you hate your job. This isn't healthy on your life force or souls' vibration. Some people are afraid to leave their job or try another one out, but sometimes taking a risk knowing that you have something to fall back on can get your energy flowing again.

Heaven also understands the need for law, order, structure, and discipline on Earth, otherwise there will be anarchy. There is a fine line between being too strict and not strict enough. Human rules and laws are enforced for a reason to keep the darkness of ego from acting out dangerously, which it's already doing. Imagine murders, rapes, severe crimes, huge theft, and vandalisms wreaking havoc and destroying Earth with no one to stop it, because human laws have been abolished, and there are no longer any law enforcement officers or a legal system in place to prevent it or reduce it. Those committing those types of dangerous heinous crimes would destroy the planet and each other in under a year. This is also why many souls on the other side incarnate from realms that consist of Wise Ones and Knights. These are the task master rule making Earth Angels. And yes, of course it is true there are corrupted lower evolved souls in charge contributing to the noise. Yet, it's the calling of the Wise Ones and Knights to keep order to a degree. This also means that a lower evolved soul will not vibe well with a soul from those realms as the Wise Ones tend to come off harsh. They're usually either extremely loved or extremely hated with no in between. The Knights have some compassion in there that tempers that harshness a bit.

You have psychic gifts that can assist yourself as well as others in a myriad of positive ways. When you tune into the vibrations from beyond and dissolve the blocks preventing the messages from coming in loud enough to grasp them, then you'll be amazed at what you pick up on. Everyone's methods of connecting with their Spirit team vary. You will discover along your journey as to what's working, what isn't, and how to navigate through that.

Through daily work, discipline, and exercises you can awaken your psychic sensitivity. It would require a lifestyle change as well as an open mind to seek out what might seem like the unknown, but it is truly home in reality to the soul. There are many avenues to take that can assist in cracking open your gifts, which are already built into each soul.

Spiritual studies have become widely accepted as the years have progressed. It's been a growing industry that incurs billions of dollars post 2000's. People are becoming more curious or interested in the genre and in wanting to gain knowledge surrounding this industry in order to help them reach a higher sense of peace.

It is true that some human souls seem to be much more in tune than others, but a great deal of that has to do with them diving into the craft regularly, and/or not allowing the practical world distractions to block them from peering through the veil efficiently.

There was a time in history that anyone believed to be psychic or a prophet, was a witch, Satan's helper, or sorcerer. They were condemned to death as a result. Even if you were considered different and set apart from society, then you were branded evil and were persecuted in some violent way. If you displayed those traits, then you were looked upon as the spawn of Satan and a blasphemous sinner. Many were killed for observing those traits either by beheading, hanging, strangulation, torturing, crucifixion, or by being burned or crushed to death. Times have significantly changed since those archaic days. Now more people are growing hip to the knowledge that all souls have these inherent God given gifts of Heavenly communication. Some are starting columns, blogs, You Tube video vlogs, social media sites, getting published, giving seminars, speeches, and on and on. Today it's celebrated when at one point in history it was shunned or forbidden. There is nothing sinful or forbidden about having a strong connection with Heaven in order to positively improve your life and the lives of others.

Even though the spiritual genre is becoming more celebrated or accepted, there are also a great many cases in some countries that have not progressed within the genre. They still observe the burning of people who seem to be *witches* during seemingly progressive times. One case involved a 20-year-old mother of two in Papua New Guinea. She was blamed for the death of a 6-year-old boy. A mob of relatives of the boy took the young mother and then stripped, tortured, and burned her alive. This was in 2013 and the world did not talk about it. How fast is Earth evolving away from that if this is still going on? Perhaps in North America or in parts of Europe that is unheard of, but there are still some countries continuing to live in the stone ages. They need to be brought up to speed, but that isn't likely to happen soon. Earth has existed for centuries and yet exuding love seems to still be an impossible feat that many have no interest in. A book like this cannot be sold in some countries because of the content. This is what happens when a soul denies it's true nature and refuses to educate itself, raise its consciousness, move forward and upward, and connect with the Divine.

The lower evolved look upon those set apart from the crowd as odd, but those with a raised consciousness and a high vibration are able to see that persons greater purpose for standing out. If you are odd, then you are more gifted with a larger purpose than you can imagine. Following the crowd is playing it safe. Those considered odd veer away from the norm because the norm needs to be changed.

While there has been a rise in atheism and anarchy as a result and side effect of the judgment that exists within organized religion, there has also been a rise of spiritualists professing to being psychically connected. This is no accident, because all souls are connected. If there is a soul energy living in an organism, plant, person, or animal, then it is psychically and energetically connected. You are also psychically and energetically connected to it too. Someone in tune to energies can hold a crystal or stone in their hand and sense the vibrations moving through it. They are aware of the movement taking place beyond the physical material life.

Psychics and Mediums who publicly profess to having a connection with the other side are simply recognizing the God given gifts within them that all are born with and that all are capable of reaching. One may not connect with the other side in the exact same way as another, but all souls have the capacity to have a strong connection with the other side.

Track your interactions with your Guides and Angels by keeping a journal of the information you receive from above. Even if you think it might be your imagination, write it down anyway. Record each message you receive, whether you believe it's from your Spirit team, your ego, or your own intuition. After a month or a period of time has passed, then revert back to it and jot down the outcome of that message. You will be able to tell the difference between the self-generated messages and the messages received from your guides. Trust the messages you receive without fear or doubt. If you make a mistake or you end up being wrong about something, big deal keep on going. Your ego will get in the way at times and create unnecessary negative self-talk that is not based in truth. Sometimes you make a mistake, but with practice you improve at focusing on what is your higher self and what is not.

Anyone can connect to the other side who works at it. You have to take care of yourself on all levels, such as physically, spiritually, mentally, and emotionally. When you have raised your vibration on those key well-being traits, then the closer you are to receiving accurate, mind-blowing, heavenly communication.

Follow the strong black and white code of spiritual ethics as your gifts develop and expand. Avoid offering random serious psychic information to someone unless you've expressly asked them if it's okay to tap into their energy. While sometimes you may automatically be tapping into their energy without trying or intending to like myself, I avoid reaching out to someone or approaching them with dangerous challenging information unless specifically asked.

A good balanced diet helps to increase psychic awareness. This isn't a fun rule for some who love their guilty pleasures and believe me I understand as I have my own personal guilty pleasures, but I do keep it in moderation. It's human nature to be attracted to fun foods. The truth is that a good deal of these guilty pleasures dim or block the psychic input entirely. You are what you eat. This popular saying is true. If you continuously eat heavy foods that are not good for you, then that weighs you down. In order to assist in increasing psychic receptivity, you need healthy foods. These are foods that give you brain power and improve your health. Because when your body, mind, and soul are operating on high capacity, then this assists in increasing the awareness to spirit reception.

Your soul at its core is a high vibrational being filled with ever flowing love, joy, and serenity. Don't forget who you are. Don't get lost in the negative toxic energy of the physical world. Take care of yourself, which means taking care of your soul and body on all levels as much as possible. Incorporate healthy life changes you can make today that will help you in awakening the parts of you that existed from the conception of your soul. These are the parts that can help you be happier, stronger, and that much more powerful.

You were born a vessel of love! Even if you do nothing with the gifts that exist within you, you will at least be shining that bright light of high vibrational energy onto all those in your path, which in turn tempers the severity of the bullets firing all over the place by the darkness of ego. The ego may have tantrums and cause all sorts of noise, but contrary to belief, love is more powerful than any other energy that exists on any plane in the end. Let your love flow and shine outwardly wherever you go. Remember to revert back to love, joy, and peace when possible. Take regular action steps that can help bring you back to this natural state of being whenever you falter on your path. Be conscious of who you are and the reservoir of gifts moving through you. This world needs more love and light in it. It is up to you to help guide others in that direction by doing the individual work to evolve and raise your consciousness. The planet doesn't need a ruler, since change starts with each individual.

BONUS SECTION

The energy center where the core clairs reside have a different chakra associated for each one. Your chakras are energy points within your souls make up where all energy flows through.

In the remaining bonus section of this book, I touch on the basic core chakras. This includes what aspects of your life they rule as well which psychic channels some of them are connected to.

This is taken from my book, *"Awaken Your Creative Spirit"*

Chapter Eleven

THE CHAKRAS

$\mathcal{A}$ Chakra *(pronounced "shock-ruh")* is an energy point within your soul's aura. There are hundreds of chakras throughout the soul and body, but there are eight core chakras that dominate. Your chakra is where God, your life force, and energy flow through. Each chakra looks like a colored spinning wheel to a clairvoyant or someone who has the ability to see the colors of one's aura. They see the individual chakra's spinning like little fans located at specific points of the body from head to toe.

Each chakra emits a different color. They spin counter clockwise and look like an oscillator fan emitting a different color out of it. When the color grows dirty, dark, or muddy, then this can indicate a problem in that area. When you experience anything negative related to what that chakra represents, then this dulls the color of the fan and changes the size of the chakra. It doesn't matter what size the chakra is. What is important is that all the chakras be relatively the same size. When one or more of the chakras are a different size than the others, then this can suggest an imbalance in a specific part of your life.

The chakras are not physical in nature, meaning it's not a human organ or something that is detectable to the human eye. The knowledge of chakras started out as a belief system in India that was eventually adopted worldwide in many spiritual or new age circles.

Each chakra represents a part of you and your life. The first three chakras are located from the pelvic area to just below the rib cage. Those chakras spin slowly representing physical external issues and circumstances. They emit a brighter joyful warmer color from red, orange, and yellow. The remaining five core chakras are located from the chest up through the top of your head. Those chakras spin much faster than the other three and represent more personal issues and circumstances. They emit a more subdued calming color from green, light blue, maroon, indigo, and violet.

Each of the core eight chakras spins quicker than the chakra below it. For example, the root chakra at the base spins slowly, while the sacral chakra above it spins slightly faster than the root chakra, and so forth.

When you negatively focus on a particular issue in your life, then this can imply that the chakra that represents the issue is dirty and off balance. When you have a dirty chakra, then this can compound the issues associated with that chakra. It also creates unevenness in your world while blocking the communication line to Heaven. This is why it's beneficial to touch on the core individual chakras. This is for those who don't know much about it or what they represent. When your chakra energy points are clear of debris and spinning at optimum levels, then this gives you greater psychic perception and input. This assists in awakening the creative spirit part of you.

In this chapter, we will briefly look at the eight core chakras starting at the bottom and moving our way up to the top so that you have a basic idea of what they represent.

ROOT CHAKRA - RED

The Root Chakra sits at the base of your spine. The root is like the root or base of a tree. When properly nourished, the roots come up from the ground and blossom into a tree, plant, or flower. The root chakra concept is much like the growth of a plant. When you nurture and take care of it, then this adds nourishment to the other chakras helping them strengthen. It is closest to the Earth and therefore connected to all things related to earthly issues and needs. This means that concerns surrounding money, security, physical desires, and wishes are all connected to the root chakra.

When you have money issues or worry about paying your bills, or you have concerns connected to your physical possessions such as your car or any material items, then this dirties up your root chakra. This also includes concerns having to do with your career and work related circumstances. If you do not feel appreciated at work, or you don't make enough money, or you have any sort of fear connected to work, career, or life purpose, then this will create an imbalance in the root chakra area.

The root chakra spins with an illumination of the color red. The stronger the red, the more activated the chakra is. When it is less activated, the color is a muddier red and the wheel putters and attempts to poorly spin around. It's like a clogged fan having a difficult time getting started.

The root chakra is connected to your physical desires. It is at the base of your spine and represents your desires for a secure firm foundation in your life. In order for a tree to grow and blossom, it must first have strong roots firmly implanted into the ground. When this is set, it begins to grow and prosper. This same concept is how the chakra's work. Ground and stabilize your root chakra, then this will help feed the other chakras.

Other signs your root chakra is unstable are when you experience fear and anxiety about your future or over anything that knocks your secure stability off kilter. When you roam through life feeling anxiety, insecure, or unsafe, then this is a sign your root chakra is dirty. Anxiety of any kind is connected to fear. Fear is connected to the root chakra. Symptoms can be chronic laziness, fatigue, anxiety, depression, anger, or irritability.

Signs that you have a strong root chakra are when you feel confident, stable, and grounded. Physical exercise or activity can help strengthen your root chakra. Keeping your body strong is of benefit to your root chakra and your overall health. Removing negative feelings of fear or insecurity in areas connected to your physical survival clears up any gunk in your root chakra. Get out in nature and plant your feet on the physical Earth to ground and stabilize your body and soul, which brightens up your root chakra.

Archangel Michael is the being to call on to assist in strengthening your root chakra. He can extract fear and insecurities from your aura and boost your confidence and optimism.

SACRAL CHAKRA - ORANGE

The Sacral Chakra is the second chakra located in the pelvic/reproductive area below the navel and slightly above the Root Chakra. It glows a bright orange when spinning at a peak level.

The sacral chakra *(pronounced Say-Krull)* is connected to your passions, sensuality, and creativity. It is what brings you joy, pleasure, and enjoyment. When you express yourself creatively, then the cleaner your sacral chakra is. If you have a healthy sex drive, or the creative part of you is fully awakened, then you have a strong sacral chakra.

Someone with perpetual addictive behavior patterns is likely to have a dirty sacral chakra.

There is a difference between a healthy sex drive and sex addiction. There is a distinction between enjoying a beer or two, and drinking a six-pack in one sitting. The enjoyment and pleasure of a glass of wine is beautiful as you soak in the valley of wine country on a hot Summer day. The opposite extreme is drinking a bottle of wine alone every night in your room to escape or push down your emotions. The addiction dirties up the sacral chakra.

Positive ways of clearing the sacral chakra are by immersing yourself into creative projects or a creative hobby. Other ways to brighten up your sacral chakra are by partaking in exercises and lifestyle choices that improve your overall well-being, emotional state, which also awaken your creative side.

The sacral chakra is also connected to your reproductive organs, not just sexually, but the organs themselves from a health and clinical perspective.

When your emotional equilibrium is all over the place and not in balance, then this can cause your sacral chakra to become clogged and dirty. You know this is the case if you find that your emotions are rising into co-dependency with anyone you come across whether it's a love relationship, friendship, or someone you're getting to know. Someone who lives for toxic drama and gossip have a muddy sacral chakra. Obsessions over food or gluttony lead to an unbalanced sacral chakra as well.

Activate your sacral chakra by partaking in

activities that bring you joy and harmony. This is pending that it is not toxic or an addiction. Take a weekend getaway trip to somewhere amazing with a loved one. Spend that time connecting and having fun together. Kiss and make passionate love to one another. Dive into a creative project or hobby. All of this brightens up, activates, and awakens your sacral chakra

Bring your life and habits to the level of passion, sensuality, joy, harmony, sexuality, and creativity in order to balance out your sacral chakra.

Archangel Jophiel and Archangel Gabriel are the higher beings to call on to assist in balancing your sacral chakra. They work by igniting your passion, sensuality, beauty, joy, and creativity essence.

SOLAR PLEXUS - YELLOW

The Solar Plexus Chakra is the third Chakra located below the navel and above the Sacral Chakra. It glows a bright yellow like the Sun when it is spinning in top form. It is linked to your power and how you express yourself. Do you express yourself through aggressiveness, passive aggressiveness, or assertiveness? This is all connected to the solar plexus chakra, which is your inner power and willpower.

Having a strong solar plexus chakra is when you are centered and balanced. Someone who reacts dramatically or with hyper emotions to circumstances does not have a strong solar plexus at that moment. You have a strong solar plexus chakra when you have a clear mind about things. You think logically, openly, and methodically. You have great drive, persistence, and ambition. You're a go getter and ensure that business is taken care of. If you want something, you get to work on figuring out how to achieve it.

You know when your solar plexus chakra is becoming dirty when you exhibit feelings of low self-esteem, or when your emotions are perpetually on the negative side and all over the place. Loving, accepting, and appreciating all that you are gives you a clear clean running solar plexus chakra.

While someone with a strong solar plexus chakra will go after what they want and are ambitious, the flipside of that and what muddies up your solar plexus chakra is when you are controlling, domineering, and egotistical. This is also someone who bullies others online or in person. It's the negative commenter on any Internet story or page.

Having a weak solar plexus chakra is also if you live in denial around an issue. You have no will power or you give your power away to others. It's when you have obsessions of being powerful or the opposite extreme where you allow others to dominate you. This can also be in the work arena where you feel victim to a toxic co-worker or boss. The toxic co-worker or boss is being egotistical or narcissistic also, which dulls the solar plexus chakra.

Igniting your inner life force gives you a robust solar plexus chakra. It is standing strong in your power and having a durable sense of confident self. It is having integrity and exuding assertiveness with your dealings with others. It is being centered and focused on getting the job done without desire for a return.

Archangel Nathaniel and Archangel Ariel are the ones to call on to assist you with your solar plexus chakra. They work to help you stand in your power, have confidence, go after what you want, and to express yourself clearly with assertive compassion.

HEART CHAKRA - GREEN

The Heart Chakra is the fourth chakra located in your physical heart and chest area. It is also in the middle of the eight core chakras blending both the physical and emotional/spiritual parts of you. It spins more rapidly than the previous three chakras illuminating a beautiful emerald green light.

As you might likely guess, the heart chakra is connected to all things having to do with love. This includes your love relationships and connections with others such as friendships, family members, acquaintances, and colleagues. If any of your connections are toxic or cause you ill will feelings, then this breaks your heart chakra.

An ex-lover has pulled a number on you leaving you saddened. You move through all of the various states of emotion from depression to anger to revenge. All of those states of emotion, while a natural reaction to having a love relationship end, also muddies up your heart chakra. This blocks love from coming in.

The heart chakra is connected to issues with all relationships from love, personal, business, to your negative states of emotion. When you cut off love and do not allow love in for fear of getting hurt or any other reason, then you clog up the heart chakra.

Ways to clean and clear the heart chakra is to remember to get back to that place where you can love again. When you forgive a partner you begin the process of cleaning the heart chakra. Perhaps they cheated on you or were abusive. Both of which are difficult to forgive or forget. Regardless, in order to clear the heart chakra of toxic debris, you must reach that place where you forgive them for yourself and your own benefit. You say, "What you did to me was not cool, but I forgive you so that I don't have to carry this pain anymore. And now I release you from my aura permanently."

The heart chakra is also connected to your Clairsentience Clair. Having a strong heart chakra awakens your Clairsentience. This is your psychic feeling sense. Activate your heart chakra by lifting your emotions and feelings to that of love, joy, and peace. This will bring on a crystal clear communication line with Heaven through Clairsentience.

Those with a strong heart chakra are warm, friendly, and open. They hold no judgment or criticism. Like the previous chakra, you can likely guess that all of those who think or post negative words and comments online have a dirty heart chakra as well.

Other ways to awaken your heart chakra are through having a healthy loving relationship, or by expressing kind words to those around you. Being supportive, loving, and partaking in self-care activates this chakra. Do things that give you a euphoric happy feeling of love, including watching a romantic comedy. Love all that you are inside and out. Love is the reason all are here and this is why having a beautiful radiating heart chakra is especially vital to your overall health and well-being.

Archangel Raphael, Archangel Haniel, or Archangel Chamuel are the hierarchy angels to call on to assist you with your heart chakra. They work with you on matters of love, healing, emotions, and attracting in high vibration connections.

THROAT CHAKRA - LIGHT BLUE

The Throat Chakra is the fifth chakra and located in your throat. It spins faster than the previous chakras while illuminating a light blue or sky blue color. The throat chakra is the area you communicate and express your thoughts. where you communicate. This includes verbally, in writing, cell phone text, or social media. Having a strong throat chakra is by expressing yourself clearly with compassion and without fear of censure. When you censure yourself or hold your thoughts and feelings in, then this affects the functioning of your throat chakra.

The throat chakra is about speaking your truth. Writers, channelers, and speakers tend to have strong throat chakras when they're working, because they are getting everything that is stuck inside them and expressing it outwardly whether on a page or to an audience. This is pending they're writing and speaking the truth without fear of being judged, criticized, or censured.

Make note of how some of the previous chakras are connected to one another. When your sacral chakra is not expressing itself through creativity, or the solar plexus chakra is preventing you from being assertive, and your heart chakra is closed up, then this can prevent you from expressing yourself with communication through your throat chakra.

If you feel as if your throat chakra has been getting dirtier, then ways to clear and cleanse it requires communicating more vocally and truthfully without fear. This doesn't mean with anger or aggression, but with assertiveness and compassion. When you communicate in a hostile manner, such as attacking others, then that dims the auric filed around the throat chakra. It's just as bad if not worse as holding your thoughts inside because you're darting that energy at others and the universe. The damage has consequences since it reaches more targets. When you hold it inside, this only hurts yourself.

Practice journaling or writing down all the things that bother you. You can write it in a journal or in an email and send it to yourself. If you wished you could've said all the things that you were thinking when your ex decided to leave you, then write it out in an email to yourself or in a journal to get it out of you. Otherwise this will squelch and tighten up your throat chakra.

Singer entertainer Shania Twain has recounted losing her voice over the years. This was due to all of the hurt, anger, anxiety, and sadness she was experiencing as her first marriage crumbled. She did not express how she was feeling and this manifested into her losing the ability to sing. Eventually, she went through some spiritual healing and forgiveness steps in a therapeutic way that resulted in assisting in re-awakening her throat chakra. This is featured in a 6-episode series called, "Why Not? With Shania Twain." It was episode 4 that takes her through the transition into opening up her voice again, which I recommend watching.

When someone is unkind and you're unable to communicate that to them out of fear or any other reason, then write it in an email to yourself, to a friend, or in a journal. Write down everything you want to say to them. You can speak as freely and as uncensored as you like since you most likely would not be sending it to them. The writing assignment is a great way to release toxins in your throat chakra while balancing it out and brightening it up.

All things having to do with communication are connected to your throat chakra. This includes speaking and communicating clearly with loved ones, friends, colleagues, acquaintances, and all you come across. Activate it by expressing your thoughts clearly and with compassion.

Archangel Gabriel is the one to call on to assist

with your Throat Chakra. She helps with communicating on all levels.

EAR CHAKRA - MAROON

The Ear Chakra is the sixth chakra and located slightly above both of your ears. It illuminates the color of Maroon (or Red Violet). This chakra is sometimes disregarded or not typically mentioned, but it is equally important. The ear chakra is a chakra that exists and affects all things connected to your hearing. This is regardless if you were born deaf or not.

Your clairaudience clear hearing channel is located in your ear chakra. When one has a strong working ear chakra, the louder the voices of spirit and Heaven come in.

The ways that the ear chakra can become muddy are by absorbing negative words being spoken by someone else to you or another. Hearing these words moves through your ear chakra and creates dust particles on it. Hearing negative words also comes from those around you in conversation. You get into an elevator where two people are complaining about work to one another, then you are absorbing the negative energy of those words through your ear chakra. Negative entertainment media such as television programs, movies, or songs can also affect the ear chakra.

The connection you have with Heaven is exceptionally strong through the ear chakra. This means someone who has no belief in the other side will tend to have a dirtier ear chakra than one who has faith. Your negative thoughts travel through your ear chakra as well so you want to be careful if you're constantly bombarding your own consciousness with the negative words of your ego.

Ways to clear your ear chakra are through intention. Visualize the bright light of Heaven being filtered through this chakra and blasting away all debris. Avoid hanging around those who are perpetually negative or gossips. Also, shut out loud irritating noises on the street such as traffic, car sounds, honking, trash cans banging, sirens, etc. All of that filters into your ear chakra and muddies it up creating a block with your clairaudience. Be mindful of the television programs you watch as you're listening to that too. When you watch movies you enjoy that have harsh negative language, then be sure to separate that from reality. Create a shield or wall between yourself and the film.

The ear chakra is in constant connection with the throat chakra. When you hear someone say something to you, it moves through your ear chakra, then when you respond in kind, the words travel out through your throat chakra.

I was born with heightened Clairaudience that ironically filters through one of my ears that was discovered to be deafer than the others when I was a kid. I was unable to pass any of the hearing tests with that ear. The irony is that the voices of my Spirit team filter loudly through that ear as if they're standing next to me.

The discs of the ear chakra are slightly above both ears and move in tandem with one another. If you hear negative words and absorb it in one ear, this affects both ear chakras at the same time. They equally receive dust particles in them in the same spot on both discs.

Archangel Zadkiel is the one to call on to assist with clearing out the toxins of your ear chakra and help you hear the voices of spirit more clearly.

THIRD EYE CHAKRA - INDIGO

The Third Eye Chakra is the seventh chakra and located between your two physical eyes, but raised just slightly above it. It spins illuminating the color of Indigo. The third eye chakra is your psychic and spiritual perception. Having a strong third eye chakra equates to having a keen Clairvoyance channel, otherwise known as clear seeing. You receive visual impressions like a mini movie playing in front of you that has significance to you or someone else. It can be what's happened, what's to come, or what's coming up. Many equate the third eye chakra to being more psychic, but the truth is that having a balanced chakra system makes one a stronger conduit with spirit. You can be highly psychic by having a strong heart chakra since that is connected to Clairsentience, and yet your third eye chakra is dimmer than the others.

Because the Third Eye is what is unseen, most are not aware of it or thinking about it. This act in itself closes up the Third Eye. Signs that your third eye chakra is opening up are seeing violet sparkles everywhere, or you're able to see the eye sitting on its side staring back at you when you close your physical eyes. You might start to have vivid dreams or you constantly see etheric images put in front of you of what's to come. You see spirits as opaque or translucent around you. Someone who is afraid of seeing spirits will cause the third eye chakra to close up.

Like the ear chakra, when one is a non-believer of anything spiritual related then this causes the third eye chakra to become dirty and shut down. The third eye chakra is the eye or window that sees what others cannot see. It is the window into the other side, spirit worlds, and dimensions that exist. When you're able to see the Third Eye, you view it sitting on its side looking right at you from within your mind. This is different than the physical eyes you were born with that view things happening in real time in front of them.

Viewing physical circumstances through your physical eyes can dim the Third Eye because you might be absorbing negative imagery in others behaviors around you. The hyper focus on what's happening around you in the physical world closes the third eye chakra. This includes obsessing over media and gossip stories. Everyone was born with a Third Eye, so even if it closes, you still have access to it as you do with all of the chakras and clair channel points.

When you fear the future or hold negatively to the past and what was done to you, then this dims the third eye chakra. Looking forward fearlessly to the future and the present, while forgiving your past will assist in opening the third eye chakra. Those with a clean third eye chakra tend to be creative beings open to all that is unseen. They paint pictures with their mind and translate it into their art. They are open spiritually and to God, Heaven, and all the spirit worlds that exist.

Archangel Raziel is the one to call on to assist in cleansing and awakening your Third Eye Chakra. He stimulates spiritual sight and assists in manifesting your visions.

CROWN CHAKRA - VIOLET

The Crown Chakra is the final and eighth chakra. It resides in your crown and slightly above the top of your head, which is also part of your aura. Your aura expands as great as six feet around your human body, which is why when someone sensitive is standing close to a toxic person, they are absorbing that person's energy from their aura. The aura changes color based on your mood and thoughts much like your Chakras. The crown chakra spins faster than any of the other chakras and illuminates a deep violet color.

The crown chakra is also connected to the third eye chakra. The Third Eye is what assists you in visualizing what you desire. The place of imagination begins in the crown chakra and in the mind with your thoughts. Those with strong

Claircognizance tend to have a cleaner crown chakra. These are the ones who operate primarily from the analytical mind. They have the gift of clear knowing. This is where the answers to problems seem to fall right through their crown out of nowhere.

Heaven communicates through all of your channels including the crown chakra. Channelers also have a high degree of Claircognizance, as they are able to access Divine input as it drops naturally through their conscious. They are then able to translate it onto the page. As messages and input travel and drop through your crown chakra, this is communicated to other Chakras throughout your body.

Claircognizance is one of my dominating Clairs next to Clairaudience. Born with the gift of knowing has enabled me to help a great many people over the course of my life. Since early childhood I have been offering others Divine wisdom regarding issues they needed help with.

Your crown chakra is associated with your overall consciousness where Divine information flows through you. When someone lacks of consciousness, such as a terrorist, someone who bullies, name calls, antagonizes others, and feels nothing, then these are people with a dirty crown chakra. They have closed up the access to the Divine.

Words and thoughts flow through the crown chakra, so practice keeping the vibration energy of those words to ones that are positive. Activate your crown chakra by diving into reading, writing, higher learning, and research endeavors. How you perceive everything, including the world around you and what is unseen, filters through the crown chakra.

Archangel Uriel is the one to call on to help in awakening the crown chakra as he rules those with Claircognizance. He guides others with his lantern filled with light down the higher path by dropping helpful insight, ideas, and wisdom into your crown chakra.

CLEANSING THE CHAKRAS

You can cleanse the chakras by moving into a calm meditative and relaxing space. Visualize each of the chakra wheels spinning counter clockwise. Then imagine God's white light shining through each of the wheels blasting away all of the dark debris latched onto these wheels. These spinning wheels are much like mini-fans. When a spinning fan has been used for quite some time it begins to collect dust on it. This is what it's like with your chakras, which is why regular maintenance is needed to keep your chakras clear from debris. You can do that with the power of visualization, or by changing your behavior and thought patterns associated with that particular chakra.

When you plague your mind of thoughts of fear or lack of money, then your Root Chakra becomes dirty. When you repress your sexuality and creativity, you clog the Sacral Chakra. When you give your power away to others, you dirty up your Solar Plexus Chakra. When you live victimized over what a past lover did to you, then you block the Heart Chakra. If you keep your thoughts to yourself and do not speak your truth, then you dirty up your Throat Chakra. If you absorb negative words and sounds around you, then your Ear Chakra becomes dusty. If you don't believe in the imagination or spiritual truth, then you block the Third Eye Chakra. And when you lack of consciousness and think negative thoughts, you muddy up your Crown Chakra. All chakras have white sparkly diamond like lights in them when they are fully functioning. The opposite of that are black and brown spots in various sizes within it. Be mindful of the energy points within your soul's body.

†

Tarot Card Meanings
Available in Paperback and E-book

Tarot Card Meanings is an encyclopedia reference guide that takes the Tarot apprentice reader through each of the 78 Tarot Cards offering the potential general meanings and interpretations that could be applied when conducting a reading, whether it be spiritual, love, general, or work related questions.

The *Tarot Card Meanings* book can assist by pointing you in the general direction of where to look. It will not give you the ultimate answers and should not be taken verbatim, as that is up to you as the reader to come to that conclusion. The more you practice, read, and study the Tarot, then the better you become.

Tarot Card Meanings avoids diving into the Tarot history, or card spreads and symbolism, but instead focuses solely on the potential meanings of a card in a reading. This is by giving you a structure to jump off of, but it is up to you to take that energy and add the additional layers to your reading, while trusting your higher self, intuition, instincts and Spirit team's guidance and messages. This is an easy to understand manual for the Tarot novice that is having trouble interpreting cards for themselves, or a Tarot reader who loves the craft and is looking for a refresher or another point of view. NOTE: The *Tarot Card Meanings* book does not include a Tarot deck.

The Essential Kevin Hunter Collection
Available in Paperback and E-book

WARRIOR OF LIGHT
Messages from my Guides and Angels

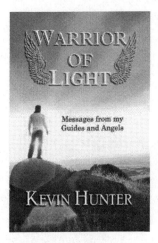

There are legions of angels, spirit guides, and departed loved ones in heaven that watch and guide you on your journey here on Earth. They are around to make your life easier and less stressful. Do you pay attention to the nudges, guidance, and messages given to you? There are many who live lives full of negativity and stress while trying to make ends meet. This can shake your faith as it leads you down paths of addictions, unhealthy life choices, and negative relationship connections. Learn how you can recognize the guidance of your own Spirit team of guides and angels around you.

Author, Kevin Hunter, relays heavenly guided messages about getting humanity, the world, and yourself into shape. He delivers the guidance passed onto him by his own Spirit team on how to fine tune your body, soul and raise your vibration. Doing this can help you gain hope and faith in your own life in order to start attracting in more abundance.

EMPOWERING SPIRIT WISDOM
A Warrior of Light's Guide
on Love, Career and the Spirit World

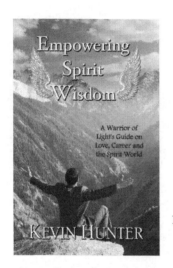

Kevin Hunter relays heavenly, guided messages for everyday life concerns with his book, *Empowering Spirit Wisdom*. Some of the topics covered are your soul, spirit and the power of the light, laws of attraction, finding meaningful work, transforming your professional and personal life, navigating through the various stages of dating and love relationships, as well as other practical affirmations and messages from the Archangels. Kevin Hunter passes on the sensible wisdom given to him by his own Spirit team in this inspirational book.

DARKNESS OF EGO

In *Darkness of Ego*, author Kevin Hunter infuses some of the guidance, messages, and wisdom he's received from his Spirit team surrounding all things ego related. The ego is one of the most damaging culprits in human life. Therefore, it is essential to understand the nature of the beast in order to navigate gracefully out of it when it spins out of control. Some of the topics covered in *Darkness of Ego* are humanity's destruction, mass hysteria, karmic debt, and the power of the mind, heaven's gate, the ego's war on love and relationships, and much more.

REACHING FOR THE WARRIOR WITHIN

Reaching for the Warrior Within is the author's personal story recounting a volatile childhood. This led him to a path of addictions, anxiety and overindulgence in alcohol, drugs, cigarettes and destructive relationships. As a survival mechanism, he split into many different "selves". He credits turning his life around, not by therapy, but by simultaneously paying attention to the messages he has been receiving from his Spirit team in Heaven since birth.

REALM OF THE WISE ONE

In the Spirit Worlds and the dimensions that exist, reside numerous kingdoms that house a plethora of Spirits that inhabit various forms. One of these tribes is called the Wise Ones, a darker breed in the spirit realm who often chooses to incarnate into a human body one lifetime after another for important purposes.

The *Realm of the Wise One* takes you on a magical journey to the spirit world where the Wise Ones dwell. This is followed with in-depth and detailed information on how to recognize a human soul who has incarnated from the Wise One Realm.

Author, Kevin Hunter, is a Wise One who uses the knowledge passed onto him by his Spirit team of Guides and Angels to relay the wisdom surrounding all things Wise One. He discusses the traits, purposes, gifts, roles, and personalities among other things that make up someone who is a Wise One.

Wise Ones have come in the guises of teachers, shaman, leaders, hunters, mediums, entertainers and others. *Realm of the Wise One* is an informational guide devoted to the tribe of the Wise Ones, both in human form and on the other side.

IGNITE YOUR INNER LIFE FORCE

Ignite Your Inner Life Force is an introduction guide for teens, young adults, and anyone seeking answers, messages, and guidance and surrounding spiritual empowerment. This is from understanding what Heaven, the soul, and spiritual beings are to knowing when you are connecting with your Spirit team of Guides and Angels.

Some of the topics covered are communicating with Heaven, working with your Spirit team, what your higher self is, your life purpose and soul contract, what the ego is, love and relationships, your vibration energy, shifting your consciousness and thinking for yourself even when you stand alone. This is an in-depth primer manual offering you foundation as you find a higher purpose navigating through your personal journey in today's modern day practical world.

AWAKEN YOUR CREATIVE SPIRIT

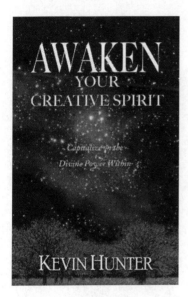

Your creative spirit is more than being artistic and getting involved in creativity pursuits, although this is a good part of it. When your creative spirit is activated by a high vibration state of being, then this is the space you create from. You can apply this to your dealings in life, your creative and artistic pursuits, and to having a greater communication line with your Spirit team on the Other Side. *Awaken Your Creative Spirit* is an overview of what it means to have access to Divine assistance and how that plays a part in arousing the muse within you in order to bring your state of mind into a happier space.

The *Warrior of Light* series of mini-pocket books are available in paperback and E-book by Kevin Hunter called, *Spirit Guides and Angels, Soul Mates and Twin Flames, Divine Messages for Humanity, Raising Your Vibration, Connecting with the Archangels, and The Seven Deadly Sins*

LOVE PARTY OF ONE
*Surviving the Pitfalls of Dating
and Relationships in a Loveless World*

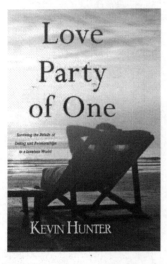

Love Party of One examines the current love and dating world and what to expect for anyone struggling with being single and longing for love.

One of the ways of surviving modern day dating and relationships in a loveless world is by armoring yourself with knowledge. This includes knowledge over the way things currently are. You've went to psychic readers, you've cast spells, you put yourself out there, did the vision boards, the crystal meditations, and other love rituals presented to you, but you still find you're desperately wishing the person of your dreams was here already. You grow cynical as if it will never happen and that you just have to accept the fact that perhaps it's not in the cards. Dating is a battlefield, be prepared to get dirty. The dating market is an equal opportunity killer and no soul is exempt from the challenges they face when it comes to love.

About the Author

Kevin Hunter is an author, love expert, and channeler. His books tackle a variety of genres and tend to have a strong male protagonist. The messages and themes he weaves in his work surround Spirit's own communications of love and respect which he channels and infuses into his writing work. His spiritually based empowerment books include  *Warrior of Light, Empowering Spirit Wisdom, Realm of the Wise One, Reaching for the Warrior Within, Darkness of Ego, Ignite Your Inner Life Force, Awaken Your Creative Spirit, The Seven Deadly Sins, Four Psychic Clair Senses,* and *Tarot Card Meanings.* He is also the author of the dating guide *Love Party of One,* the horror/drama, *Paint the Silence,* and the modern day erotic love story, *Jagger's Revolution.* Before becoming an author, Kevin started out in the entertainment business in 1996 as the personal development guy to one of Hollywood's most respected talent, Michelle Pfeiffer, for her boutique production company, Via Rosa Productions. She dissolved her company after several years and he made a move into coordinating film productions for the big studios on such films as *One Fine Day, A Thousand Acres, The Deep End of the Ocean, Crazy in Alabama, The Perfect Storm, Original Sin, Harry Potter & the Sorcerer's Stone, Dr. Dolittle 2,* and *Carolina.* He considers himself a beach bum born and raised in Southern California. For more information, www.kevin-hunter.com